Garden
Accents

S

EN

EN

ALEXANDRIA, VIRGINIA

Garden Accents

Introduction

It is fun to wander through a garden, discovering its secrets and treasures—a small vine-covered tower, a sculpture standing in a clearing, a bench tucked away off a path awaiting a visitor. Creating these magical touches is part of the art of garden design. You'll be surprised at the marvelous things you can make with just a few tools, some common building materials, and a can-do attitude.

The projects in this book were developed to add some of that sense of magic to your garden. They were also designed to be built by people with a limited amount of experience in making things. While the designs may look sophisticated, the underlying construction is always quite simple. The individual pieces are, for the most part, off-the-shelf items. Connections are made with nails, screws, and bolts, not intricate wood joinery. And the tools you'll need are ones you probably already have—hammers, drills, saws, screwdrivers, and so on.

Before you begin a project, study it carefully so you are familiar with the way the pieces go together. The step-by-step photos will guide you through the entire process, and the cutting lists will tell you exactly how big to make the pieces. Most of all, enjoy! 🌼

Getting Started

While you can purchase something similar to many of the items featured in this book, it is more gratifying to furnish your garden with accents you have made yourself. If you already have some do-it-yourself or woodworking experience under your belt, you know what fun it is to show off your latest project. If you are new to the process of "making," what better place to start than by building something for your beloved garden?

As you page through this book, take notice of which projects seem like they would be fun to make and would find a perfect spot in your garden. Then read through the step-by-step sequences and note what tools and techniques are involved. Compare these to the tools and skills you already possess. If your toolbox is a little light, you may decide it is worth acquiring a new piece of equipment, or you may be able to borrow an item from a friend. If it is experience you lack, start with some of the smaller items, or else just dive right in and learn as you go. Don't be afraid to make a few practice cuts, or to modify the way something is made to better suit your tools and abilities. ❧

Developing a Plan

Choosing the right accent for the right place in your garden is as important as choosing the proper plants for a border or the perfect tree for a bed. Ideally, you would be able to plan a garden from scratch, choosing both the plants and the accents to complement each other—a process similar to redecorating a room with entirely new furniture, carpeting, artwork, and so on. But how often do you have such an opportunity? In reality, garden design, like interior design, is an evolutionary process. You start with certain things, then add to and replace them as time goes on. The end result (if there ever really is one) is a gradual but often quite dramatic transformation.

During the evolutionary process, you constantly have to consider how well the parts fit together. As you look at the projects in this book, try to envision them in your garden. Think about their scale, color, and overall look. If necessary, use cardboard boxes or other props to help you visualize the end result. Once you decide what items to include, list them in order of importance. Next, look at the materials involved in each project. You may save money and time by building certain accents at the same time if, for example, two projects will each require half a sheet of plywood.

PLANNING AHEAD

Once you decide what to build, go over the project to make sure you understand how it goes together. Following the sequence presented here will help you get ready for the actual construction. If you encounter steps or techniques that you are unfamiliar with, read about the relevant topics in this introductory section for helpful instructions and tips. Be sure to check the Have on Hand list carefully and make any necessary adjustments based on your available tools and materials, as well as the dimensions of the project you would like to make. ❧

HAVE ON HAND:

▶ Tape measure

▶ Pencil

▶ Graph paper

▶ Eraser

▶ Straightedge

▶ Magazine photos for ideas

▶ Seed catalogs

▶ Paint color cards

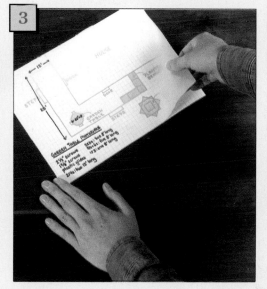

For a large project, start by measuring its intended location to make sure it will fit. If not, you may need to modify the design.

Make a quick drawing of your idea to work out the general sizes and relationships of the parts. Use graph paper and a ruler as aids.

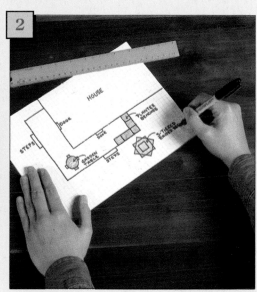

Add dimensions to the drawing, based on your measurements. From these dimensions, develop a materials list, stating the size of all the parts.

If you can't find a material you want locally, lumberyards can special-order an amazing variety of materials.

Building a Basic Tool Kit

MEASUREMENT AND LAYOUT

It pays to get accurate measuring tools, as accurate layouts are critical for doing precise work.

TAPE MEASURE
For most work, a 12-foot model is adequate. For larger projects, a 25-foot tape is handy.

SQUARES
Get a framing square for laying out cuts on plywood. A speed square or combination square is better for use on smaller pieces of wood.

HAND TOOLS

To build the projects in this book, you'll need these basic hand tools.

HAMMER
A basic, 16-ounce claw hammer is adequate for all nailing chores. For smaller nails, a 12-ounce hammer may be easier to use.

SCREWDRIVERS
Get both Phillips and straight blades. Try to match the size of the driver to the screw to avoid damaging the screwhead.

POWER TOOLS

While you will be able to build all the projects in this book with hand tools, there are a few power tools that can do the job much faster.

CIRCULAR SAW
This saw is very useful for cutting boards to the right length and for cutting up pieces of plywood. It can also rip boards to the right width.

SABER SAW
This saw doesn't cut as quickly as a circular saw, but it is capable of cutting curves.

Checking a Square

One easy way you can improve the accuracy of your work is to make sure your square tool is actually square. Try this simple test. If your square passes, great. If not, consider investing in a new one. 🌸

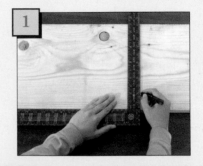

1

Find a board with a good, straight edge. Hold your square against the edge of the board and draw a line across the board's face.

SLIDING T-BEVEL AND PROTRACTOR

A T-bevel (or "bevel-square") is used for transferring angles. Use the protractor to determine the exact angle.

COMPASS

This is used for drawing circles. For large-diameter circles, use a length of string tied to a pencil.

CHALK LINE

A chalk line is a length of string coated with chalk. To use it, stretch the string between the endpoints of the line you want and pluck it to mark the line.

UTILITY KNIFE

This is a useful tool for many different tasks. Buy some extra blades so you'll always have a sharp one handy.

WRENCHES AND SOCKETS

An adjustable wrench is all that you really need, but a set of sockets can make many jobs easier.

BLOCK PLANE

A sharp block plane can save a lot of time when trimming pieces or knocking sharp corners off a piece of wood.

SCREW GUN/DRILL

The battery-powered screw gun/drill makes life much easier, especially during installations. You'll also need a set of drill bits and a few driver bits.

ELECTRIC DRILL

If you don't have a cordless drill, a regular electric drill will work. It is often handy to have two drills so you won't have to constantly change bits.

TABLE SAW

Table saws are very useful for ripping wood to the right width and cross-cutting it to length, especially if you have a lot of pieces to cut.

Flip the square over and draw a second line on top of the first.

If your square is accurate, the two lines should appear as one. If they don't, the angle between the lines is twice the amount the square is off.

Working with Power Tools

For making straight cuts to a line, a circular saw is the tool to use. A mainstay of the residential carpenter, this hand-held power tool makes quick work of most common cutting tasks. For general work where you don't have to cut pieces to a precise dimension, you can draw a line on your stock, then cut to the line by simply watching where the saw is going. When you do cut, be careful to keep the saw going straight. If you accidentally make a curved cut, the blade will probably bind and the saw will complain about it. At worst, the saw will kick back out of the cut, which can be quite dangerous, so keep a firm grip on the saw to keep it under control.

When working with a circular saw, you should definitely wear safety glasses and hearing protection. Keep both hands on the saw as you are cutting whenever you possibly can. Be aware that the blade is sticking out of the bottom side of the work, so you don't want to work directly above a surface that should not be cut. Try to keep your blade sharp—a dull blade will not cut as cleanly or accurately as a sharp one.

For accurate and safe cuts with a circular saw, it is essential to be set up properly before you pull the trigger to start the saw's motor. After you draw the lines you're cutting to, measure them again to be sure the wood will end up the correct length. If you cut off an extra half-inch, you can't put it back later! Whenever possible, firmly clamp down your workpiece and any guides to keep them from shifting after the saw has begun cutting. ❧

HAVE ON HAND:

- ▶ Circular saw
- ▶ Tape measure
- ▶ Pencil
- ▶ Chalk line
- ▶ Speed square
- ▶ Straightedge
- ▶ Clamps
- ▶ Edge guide
- ▶ Safety glasses
- ▶ Hearing protection

SAFETY TIP. *Keep your saw blade retracted as far as possible. Set the saw so the spaces between the saw teeth just clear stock thickness.*

FOR MORE ACCURATE CROSSCUTS. *Draw a line to lay out the cut. Then guide the saw along the line, using a speed square as a fence.*

FOR FAIRLY ACCURATE CUTS. *Draw a line on your stock and follow it with the saw. Try to keep the blade to the waste side of the line.*

DRAWING LONG LINES. *Use a chalk line to draw long lines quickly and accurately. Mark ends of line, stretch string tight, and snap to mark.*

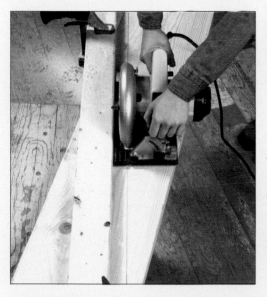

FOR MORE ACCURATE LONG CUTS. *Clamp a straight piece of wood parallel to the cut line. Run the saw along this edge.*

TO CUT NARROWER BOARDS. *Use an edge guide. If your saw doesn't have one, clamp a piece of scrap to its underside.*

HERE'S HOW

MAKING CURVED CUTS

To cut along a curve, the tool you need is a saber saw. To make the cut, draw the line of the curve on your stock, then follow the line with the saber saw. A sharp blade will be easier to guide than a dull one. Most of the better saws use what is called orbital cutting action. This means that the saw blade moves slightly forward and back in addition to up and down. The back-and-forth motion makes the saw cut faster, but it can also create more splinters. If your stock splinters badly, decrease the orbital action, or try putting a piece of masking tape along the cut line.

CUTTING WITH A TABLE SAW

If you have a lot of repetitive cuts to make, either ripping boards to the same width or crosscutting them to length, a table saw is the best tool for the job. It will enable you to get consistent results for the same task much more easily than with a circular saw or a saber saw. Unfortunately, a table saw can also be a dangerous tool, especially in the hands of an inexperienced user. If you are not sure how to use a table saw, get someone who does know how to show you the proper technique.

As with all power tools, be sure to wear hearing and eye protection whenever you are cutting on the table saw. If you are ripping a board to width (cutting along the length of a board), make sure the saw has a splitter—a thin piece of steel that sticks up behind the blade and keeps the kerf (the opening of the saw cut) from pinching closed around the blade. If the kerf pinches the blade, the board can be thrown right back at you. The splitter is not required when crosscutting (cutting across the width of a board). The blade guard should be used for both types of cut.

Besides using the blade guard as a safety feature, you also must be very careful in how you push a board through the blade. Use your left hand to control the piece, making sure never to allow your hand to get too close to the spinning blade. Push the stock through with your right hand, and use a push stick to move the piece whenever the end of the board gets within a foot of the blade.

With any saw, a sharp blade is necessary for a neat, safe cut. Duller blades are more likely to bind during cutting, and they can even burn the edges of the wood as the blade strains to cut through it. ✿

HAVE ON HAND:

▶ Table saw

▶ Tape measure

▶ Square

▶ Push sticks

▶ Clamp

▶ Scrap wood

▶ Safety glasses

▶ Hearing protection

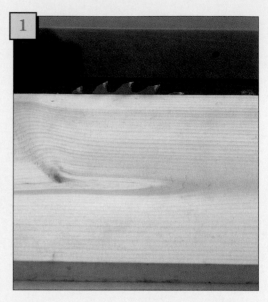

Start by setting the height of the blade. Adjust it so the spaces between the teeth just clear the top of the board you want to cut.

To rip a board to width, *set fence the correct distance from blade. Double-check the distance by measuring from blade to fence.*

To crosscut a board, *hold it securely against the miter gauge and push it past the blade. The rip fence should be pushed far out of the way.*

To crosscut several pieces to the same length, *attach a piece of scrap with a stop block at its far end to the miter gauge.*

Stand to the left of the blade. Push the board against the fence with your left hand. Push the board into the cut with your right.

To finish the cut, push the board past the blade with a push stick. To be safe, move your left hand away from the action.

HERE'S HOW

MAKING ACCURATE CUTS

Before making a cut on the table saw, check to make sure your saw is properly adjusted. The blade should be square to the table. The fence should be parallel to the blade or, if you are crosscutting, the miter gauge should be square to the blade. Properly adjusting the table saw will not only make your cuts more accurate, it will also lessen the danger of a board binding or kicking back. Once the table saw is properly set up, make a test cut in a piece of scrap. Check to make sure that the scrap has been cut straight and square, and adjust the saw if necessary.

Caring for Your Tools

If you want your tools to perform at their best and last for years, you need to invest a little time in caring for them each time you use them. This need not take long: a couple of seconds to clean away the sawdust rather than simply tossing your saw back in its case, another second or two to put your chisels back in their sleeves instead of storing them loose in your toolbox, and so on. Try to make these things a habit, almost an automatic ritual when you finish working, and you'll be pleasantly surprised at the results. You won't have to waste time hunting for missing parts or sharpening tools prematurely because they were damaged in storage.

For power and machine tools, such as drills and table saws, be sure to clean off any sawdust or wood chips before heading out of the workshop. You may find that a shop vacuum is handy for cleanup, especially for getting to the hard-to-reach corners of larger machine tools. Whenever you can, put your hand power tools back in their cases and place covers over your machine tools. This will help to keep your tools free of dust and safe from damage.

A big part of taking care of your tools is simply having a well-organized place to put them away when you are finished using them. If you have a place you can set up as a shop, you may want to build a tool panel where you can hang your tools. If you have to keep your tools stored away when they are not in use, it is a good idea to invest in several medium-sized toolboxes (large boxes tend to be too heavy to lift when loaded with tools) rather than making do with cardboard cartons or buckets. Try to keep similar tools and those used for the same type of job together, and store the accessories that go with your power tools right with the tools. Use smaller boxes inside the main box to keep track of small pieces and parts.

HAVE ON HAND:

- Rags
- Oil or lubricating spray
- Protective covers
- Toolboxes
- Dust brush

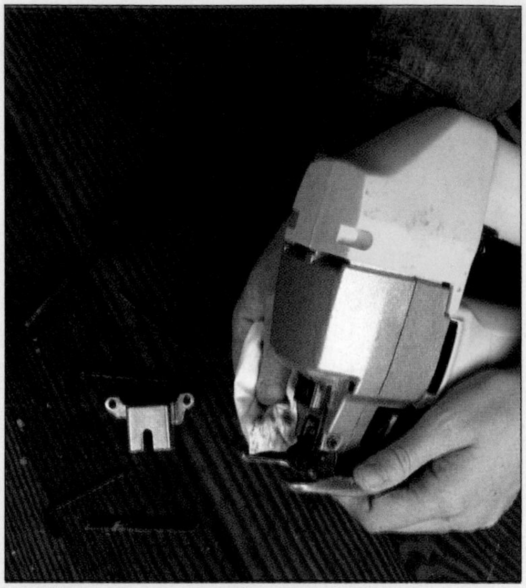

THOROUGH CLEANUP. *When you are finished with your tools, disassemble and clean them so they will be ready for the next use.*

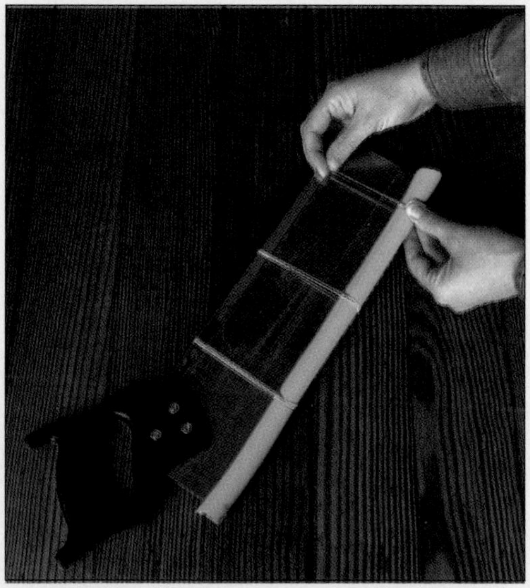

PROTECTING SAW BLADES. *If you carry saws in a toolbox, cover teeth with vinyl tubing held in place by a few rubber bands.*

POWER TOOL STORAGE. *Wrap the cord neatly around tool; store in its box along with all the blades, wrenches, and accessories.*

PROTECT SHARP EDGES. *This helps keep tools sharp and helps prevent you from accidentally cutting yourself.*

CLEANING TOOLS. *Clean dirty tools thoroughly. Spray blades and mechanism with lightweight oil. Wipe with a clean rag.*

MEASURING DEVICES. *Tools like squares need extra care to ensure that they stay accurate. Use a separate toolbox to keep them safe.*

HERE'S HOW

A PLACE FOR EVERYTHING

Pegboard makes a great tool panel, and you can purchase hooks for it that are specifically designed to hold tools. If you decide to make a tool panel, go an extra step and make plywood silhouettes for each tool and paint them a bright color. Hang the silhouettes behind the tools on the panel to indicate which tool goes where. You'll also be able to tell at a glance when a tool is missing.

SHARPENING A BLADE

Chisels and block planes are incredibly useful tools, but all too often they end up in the bottom of a toolbox because they "don't work right." Quite often the reason they don't work right is because they are not sharp. Edge tools, such as planes and chisels, do not come from the store with their blades sufficiently sharpened. Sure, they may be able to cut your finger, but they are really too dull for slicing away a thin shaving of wood. With a dull tool, you will have to exert more pressure on the tool to achieve a worse result than you would if the tool was properly sharpened. Sharpening is something you need to be sure to take care of yourself.

If you look in a woodworking catalog, you are likely to see a bewildering array of sharpening devices. And if you ask several woodworkers for advice, you'll get a different answer from each. What it comes down to is this: There is no one right way to sharpen, and there are many products available that will produce a sharp edge. If you are planning to use chisels and planes on a regular basis for fine woodworking, you may want to investigate the advantages and drawbacks of the wide variety of available sharpening products such as grinding wheels, oilstones, and waterstones.

If you are intending to use chisels and planes only occasionally for jobs such as trimming a piece for a better fit, and if you don't have any sharpening equipment, the method shown here is a good place to start. It is cheap, fast, and effective. Once you have sharpened your tools, you'll be amazed at how much better they work—and how much less of an effort you have to exert yourself. 🌿

HAVE ON HAND:

▶ Plate glass

▶ Wet-dry sandpaper

▶ Water

▶ Rags

▶ Oil

Squirt a little water on a piece of plate glass and lay a piece of wet-dry sandpaper on it. The suction from the water holds it in place.

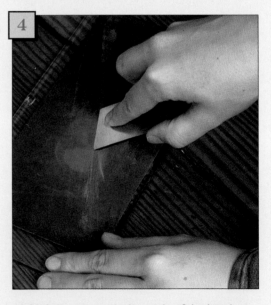

Hold the cutter up at the angle of the bevel, as though you want to take a slice out of the glass. Use forward strokes to polish the bevel.

The first time you sharpen a tool, such as the cutter of a plane, spend time polishing the flat side (back) to remove all the grinding marks.

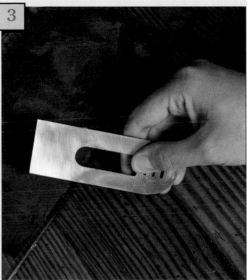

The back is done when it has an almost mirror-like shine. From now on, you'll have to give the back only a brief polish.

After the bevel is polished, give the back a few strokes on your finest sandpaper to remove any burrs that sharpening may have created.

Before reassembling the plane, spray the cutter with lightweight oil. Wipe with a clean rag.

HERE'S HOW

SHARPENING OTHER TOOLS

Chisels, knives, and plane blades aren't the only tools that benefit from sharpening. Shovels, hoes, and even screwdrivers can all benefit from a little attention. Take a look at your tools the next time you use them. If the edges are blunted from contact with too many rocks or prying open too many paint cans, try dressing up their edges with a file. You'll be amazed at what a difference smoothing away the inevitable dings can make. Be sure to hold the tool securely in a vise while you are working on it.

Choosing Materials

The projects in this book were designed to use the various materials that are readily available at most lumberyards and home centers. This includes various widths of 2-inch lumber (such as 2 x 4s), several widths of 1-inch lumber, concrete, and the occasional piece of plywood. As many of the projects are destined to sit outside, you'll need to choose your materials with care and paint or finish them, if necessary, to keep them from rotting. Between the effects of moisture and sunlight, the outside environment is a harsh place for anything made of wood.

Woods that are resistant to rot, such as cedar, are also more expensive. It may be worth the extra money to buy rot-resistant wood that doesn't require a finish, however, when you consider the time and money that you would spend painting or finishing wood such as pine.

With longevity in mind, you might be tempted to use pressure-treated lumber for everything. But this isn't the best way to go. Pressure-treated (PT) lumber has its uses, but it has drawbacks as well. For one thing, it is toxic, so you need to take extra precautions when handling and working with it. Also, PT wood is often wet when it is sold and often warps and cracks as it dries. And, if it is wet, it won't hold paint well until it dries completely. The best solution is to use PT wood only where it is most needed, such as for parts that will be in constant contact with the ground, and to use other materials whenever possible.

Whatever materials you decide to use, make sure that they blend in well with your garden, deck, and home. Naturally weathered cedar or brightly painted pine or rough-textured concrete will each provide a different color and mood to your garden landscape.

HAVE ON HAND:

▶ Tape measure

▶ Material safety data sheet (MSDS)

▶ Dust mask

▶ Work gloves

PRESSURE-TREATED WOOD. *This holds up well outside. It must be handled with care: Avoid breathing the sawdust, and wash up well.*

SYNTHETIC LUMBER. *This relatively new product is made from recycled plastic and wood fiber. It is impervious to weathering.*

CEDAR AND CYPRESS. *These naturally rot-resistant woods can be expensive but are nice to work with and look quite good.*

REGULAR FRAMING LUMBER. *Pine or spruce is an economical choice, but both require paint or other protective finish to last.*

EXTERIOR-GRADE PLYWOOD. *If your project calls for plywood, make sure you purchase plywood that is rated for exterior use.*

SCRAP PILE. *Before you go shopping, check through your pile of scraps to see if you already have any of the necessary materials.*

HERE'S HOW

PRESSURE-TREATED WOOD

Working with PT wood requires some special precautions. Wear a tight-fitting, high-quality dust mask when cutting and otherwise making dust. The average nuisance mask is not adequate. Remove your work clothes before entering your house, and wash them separately to avoid contaminating the rest of the laundry. Wash your hands and face thoroughly before eating, drinking, or smoking, and shower when you are done for the day. Dispose of any scraps and dust in accordance with local regulations. Do NOT burn or bury them.

SELECTING YOUR STOCK

When you go to your local home center or lumberyard, it pays to take a little time to select the best materials you can. You might think that all the 2 x 4s in the bin are the same, but in most cases there will be some good ones, some bad ones, and even some that are just about unusable.

Pine boards are divided into different grades, ranging from clear, straight boards, often at a hefty price, to much cheaper boards that may be twisted or riddled with knots. For exterior use, where wood is often given a solid coat of paint, you probably can purchase one of the less expensive grades, as blemishes and solid knots will be covered up.

No matter what grade of lumber you're buying, you should examine each piece and think about the parts you need to cut from it before you add it to your cart. If you need several short lengths, you may be able to use a board that is slightly bowed, as cutting it up will make

the bow much less of a problem. If a board has a check (a lumberman's term for a crack) at one end, you still may be able to use it if the piece you need is shorter than the entire length of the board. Watch out for boards that are missing part of an edge (what is called waned) or have large, loose knots. Check to see whether a board is twisted by taking it out of the stack, picking up one end, and looking down along one long edge. You may have to look at a dozen or so boards to find the two or three that you need.

For many of the projects in this book, the Have on Hand box includes a listing of the boards you need, and an additional Cutting List details the size of pieces to cut from those larger pieces. Make sure when you purchase larger boards that you will be able to cut the smaller pieces on the Cutting List from them without having to include a noticeable defect on your finished project.

After you have made your selections, be sure to put the remaining stack back together as neatly as you can. One of the reasons so many of the boards in a bin are defective is that other customers don't treat them very well. 🌸

HAVE ON HAND:

▶ Tape measure   ▶ Lumber crayon

▶ Shopping list   ▶ Straightedge

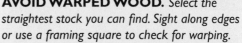

AVOID WARPED WOOD. *Select the straightest stock you can find. Sight along edges or use a framing square to check for warping.*

DISCOUNTS. *To make small items, such as this birdhouse, warped boards may be fine, as the warp is less obvious, but ask for a discount!*

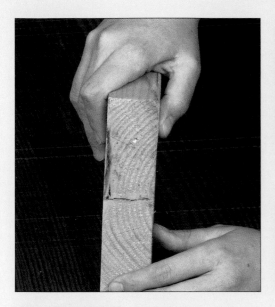

AVOID CRACKS. *Check each piece of lumber for any significant cracks. Look at the ends, as well as around any knots.*

OTHER DEFECTS. *You may notice knot-holes or irregularities on boards cut near the outside of a log or on the outside of the bundle.*

IDENTIFY BY USE. *When you buy a board, mark the part you plan to cut from it right on the board with a lumber crayon or pencil.*

BEWARE OF STAPLES. *Lumberyards often use staples to hold price tags on boards. Remove tags and staples before cutting.*

HERE'S HOW

KEEPING TRACK

If you're buying a lot of lumber at one time, it can be tricky to keep track of which board you intend to use for which part of a project. You also may want to find boards with sections that are free of knots or defects and long enough to cut out specific parts. Carry a lumber crayon or soft pencil with you as you shop. Then, as you make your selections, mark each board or section of board with the purpose it is intended for.

Choosing Hardware

You should put just as much care into selecting the hardware for your projects as you do into selecting the other materials you'll be using. The outdoor environment can cause metal to rust just as easily as it causes exposed wood to rot. Fortunately, with the increased popularity of wooden decks, home centers are now starting to stock a much more extensive selection of weather-resistant fasteners and hardware.

What you are looking for is hardware that is made of a metal that resists corrosion or that has been given a tough, weather-resistant coating. The least expensive choice is galvanized steel. You'll recognize it by its rough, dull-gray appearance. Solid brass hardware is more costly but has a nicer look to it. (Don't be fooled by the brass-plated steel used for interior hardware, as it won't hold up outside.) If you have access to a store that caters to boatbuilders, you may also find marine hardware made of bronze, which weathers very well. At the top end of the scale—both in durability and in cost—is hardware made of stainless steel; these items will provide superior service.

Whatever type of hardware you decide to use, you will save a lot of time and money if you plan ahead and buy a sufficient quantity of the sizes and varieties of screws and nails you will need to use over several different projects. Nothing wastes more time than having to run to the hardware store for those four 3-inch galvanized screws that you absolutely need. Another great timesaver is to keep your many different sizes of hardware separated neatly in their own compartments in a storage box. You already may own those 3-inch screws, but it won't matter if they are lost at the bottom of a coffee can full of screws, nuts, and bolts of undetermined sizes and styles. 🍀

HAVE ON HAND:

▶ Parachute bag

▶ Cabinet for small parts

▶ Bread pan

▶ Film canisters

▶ Coffee cans

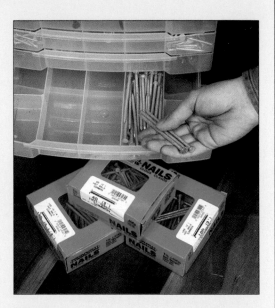

STOCKING UP ON NAILS. *It is worth buying a variety of nails if you build often. Start with a box each of 4d, 8d, 12d, and 16d.*

STAINLESS STEEL HARDWARE. *For ultimate weather resistance, try these specialized fasteners, available at many home centers.*

To keep all your different fasteners organized, try storing them in a parachute bag. These bags have a number of compartments and hold a fair amount of screws and nails in one convenient package. They are equipped with drawstrings so you can pull them closed for transport.

AN ASSORTMENT OF SCREWS. *Keep a number of different length screws on hand, including 1¼, 1⅝, 2, 2½, and 3 inches.*

OUTDOOR HINGES. *Look for hinges that have been galvanized or are made of solid brass for the best weather resistance.*

ZINC-PLATED HARDWARE. *Zinc should be given a coat or two of high-quality enamel paint for better wear.*

LOOK AROUND. *Explore your local hardware store to see what's available. You may find the fixture you're looking for in many styles.*

Working with Concrete

Set the bag of concrete mix in your mixing container. Break the bag open with the corner of your hoe, pull out the bag, and discard it.

As materials for outdoor projects go, it is hard to beat concrete. It is relatively cheap and tough; it is extremely weather resistant; it doesn't need paint or other maintenance; and you can build a form to create just about any shape you need. To work successfully with concrete, it helps to have some understanding of what concrete actually is.

Concrete is a composite of four basic ingredients: fine aggregate (sand), coarse aggregate (stone), Portland cement, and water. The fine and coarse aggregates make up the bulk of the mix; the cement serves as a binder, holding everything together; and the water serves as an activator for the cement.

Note that while most of the water used initially to hydrate the mix eventually evaporates out, a certain amount of water remains in the concrete even after the concrete is fully cured. Using too much water at the start will result in a weaker final product.

You can purchase the ingredients individually and mix the concrete yourself, taking care to use the proper proportions of ingredients for the job at hand. For most small jobs, however, it is much easier to buy prebagged concrete. Premixed concrete is sold in bags ranging from 11 to 94 pounds (94 pounds equal 1 cubic foot of concrete mix). This is usually available in two types: gravel mix and sand mix. The gravel mix is stronger and is good for projects that are fairly thick. The sand mix leaves out the coarse aggregate, which makes it somewhat weaker, but it is easier to cast into thin sections. ❧

HAVE ON HAND:

▶ Concrete mix

▶ Wheelbarrow or mortar box

▶ Hoe

▶ Shovel

▶ Small concrete trowel

▶ Water

▶ Forms

Add a little more water as you mix. It is a lot easier to add water than it is to add more cement, so proceed slowly.

Add water gradually, just enough to wet down the mix, but not so much that it forms puddles. You can always add more water if needed.

Mix in the water with a hoe. A mason's hoe has two holes in the blade, but a garden hoe will work just as well.

HERE'S HOW

MIXING CONCRETE

The first time you mix concrete, add the water extremely slowly to make sure you don't use too much. Have all your tools and forms ready before you start mixing. Concrete can start to set very quickly, especially on a hot day, so you do not want to delay once you add the water. Be very careful as you open the bags. Portland cement is caustic and will burn your eyes if it gets in them.

Keep mixing until the concrete mix is thoroughly wet, but not runny. The concrete should have a "fluffy" texture.

Trowel the concrete into the corners of the form first, to make sure they are completely filled. Then fill in the rest of the form with a shovel.

Building Planters and Trellises

Growing plants on trellises and in planters can add another entire dimension to your gardening. Trellises add height to an otherwise flat landscape. In fact, a three-dimensional trellis, such as the vining tower shown on page 46, can become the focal point of a garden, rising from the center of a low-lying area. Flat trellises, such as the one on page 42, can dress up blank walls, adding color and texture to an otherwise bland surface. And trellises can help make the best use of every square inch of space in a tight plot, allowing you to grow vegetables such as beans and cucumbers in a small area.

Planters, on the other hand, allow you to move your garden up out of your beds and onto your deck, porch, or even into your home. They also allow gardening on a small scale—just the thing if you live in an apartment and lack the space for a more extensive project. Almost any container can be pressed into service as a planter—in fact, many of the projects presented here make use of the plastic containers that are readily available at garden centers. Lining a wooden planter with a plastic container keeps the soil and moisture away from the wood, which will help the planter to last longer.

Making a Small Cedar Planter

Even if you live in a city apartment, a small planter like this one can bring a little of nature's beauty close to home. Make just one planter to brighten a humble urban balcony, or enough to create a floral symphony under the windows of a home in the country. Whichever approach you choose, feel free to modify the planter to suit your situation and finish it to match your home. The planter shown is built of rough-sawn cedar, which lends a rustic look to the project.

The planter is actually a wooden cover for a standard plastic window box, which is available in a variety of lengths from most garden centers. Using a wooden cover around a plastic box has several advantages. First, it prevents rot by keeping the soil and moisture away from the wood. It also allows you to remove the box for planting, tending to the soil, and protecting plants from cold weather. You may even want to keep several boxes going at once, swapping them in and out of the planter as different flowers come into bloom. And finally, while plastic planters work fine on their own, a wooden planter is much nicer, especially if you customize it to suit your décor. ❧

BUILDING THE PLANTER

Construction of the planter is fairly straightforward and shouldn't take more than an hour or two. Cut the pieces to size, then screw them together. If you're using cedar to build the planter, try to find rustproof screws that are not galvanized. Galvanized screws will react with the cedar and leave dark streaks on your planter. ❧

HAVE ON HAND:

- ► Tape measure
- ► Circular saw
- ► T bevel
- ► Coping saw or saber saw
- ► Screw gun/drill and bits
- ► 2-inch deck screws
- ► 32-inch ready-made plastic window box
- ► 8-foot-long 1 x 10 cedar board

Cutting List:

- ► Two sides: ¾ x 6½ x 31⅛ inches
- ► Two ends: ¾ x 8 x 9½ inches
- ► Four supports: ¾ x 1 x 8⅛ inches

Cut the sides to size. Set your T-bevel to match the slope of the end of the plastic box. Lay out this angle on both ends of both sides.

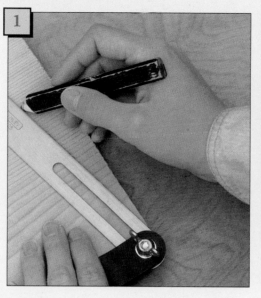

Cut on the waste sides of the lines with a circular saw. Keep the wide part of the saw base on the side, allowing the cutoff to drop free.

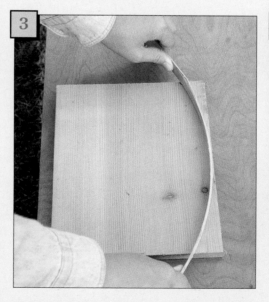

Cut the ends to size. Then have a helper bend a thin scrap of wood that you can trace to lay out the curved cuts.

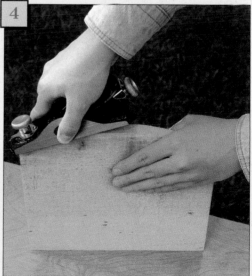

Cut along the curved lines with a coping saw. Use sandpaper or a block plane to smooth away the saw marks and true the curves.

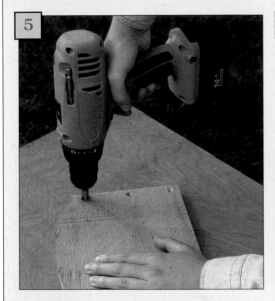

To keep wood from splitting, drill holes for the screws with a 3/32-inch drill bit. Countersink holes as shown, then screw ends to the sides.

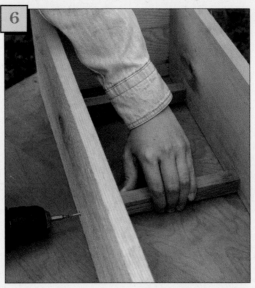

Set a support 3 inches from each end and flush with the bottom. Space remaining supports equally and screw in place.

To permanently install the planter, mount it on a wooden rail with screws driven down through the supports.

Drill a few holes in the bottom of the plastic window box for drainage. Drop the box inside the planter to finish the job.

HERE'S HOW

BOX UNDER A WINDOW

If you want to use this planter as a true window box, you'll need to mount it to the side of your house. The trick here is to keep the mounting from allowing moisture to penetrate into the house. Rather than simply screwing the unit to the wall, attach a mounting strip to the wall first, caulking the fasteners well. Then attach the wooden box to the strip. This provides a little air space behind the box, preventing moisture from building up behind it.

Alternatives

DETAILS TIE IT ALL TOGETHER

Depending on the equipment and tools you have available, you can make your window boxes or railing planters as elaborate or as simple as you like. For inspiration, look to the trim on your house. Try to pick up on some of the molding profiles and other architectural details around the doors and windows or along the edges of the roof. If you have a router, you can use it to re-create these profiles on your planter. Or check out the selection of moldings at your local home center or lumberyard.

On the planter shown here, the front panel was rabbeted to form the raised field in the center. The trim pieces around the top and bottom of the planter, along with the end pieces, make up a frame for this simple detail, creating a charming effect. These trim pieces also serve to hold the plastic liner in place.

Underneath, a pair of graceful, curved brackets supports the planter against the wall. These two-piece brackets are screwed to the side of the house. Attaching the planter in this manner allows you to leave a little space for air circulation between the house and the planter, which will help prevent mildew and rot. ❧

PORTABLE PLANTERS

There's no rule that says a window box or railing planter has to remain attached under a window or astride a railing. With the right stand, such a planter becomes a piece of porch furniture that can be used to enhance an outdoor ensemble or brighten a shady patio. Rather than having to gaze out at your garden, you can have a little bit of greenery right next to your favorite chair. With a little thought to your color scheme, you may even be able to entice hummingbirds or butterflies to fly up close. These delightful creatures are attracted to red and purple, so choose plants whose flowers come in those hues. Salvia, zinnias, and impatiens all do well in planters and have blossoms in the appropriate colors.

If you would like to create your own movable feast of color, you can build a simple stand for the planter shown on the previous pages, or you can purchase a stand from your local garden center. A number of manufacturers also make planters that are designed to use plastic window boxes as liners. Here a lovely bunch of yellow daffodils and red snapdragons grace a wicker planter chosen to complement the ensemble of wicker furniture on the porch. ❧

Building a Patio Planter

You don't have to own an expanse of land to be a gardener. Even a small urban balcony or a townhouse deck can come alive with the addition of a few plants. While you can settle for a selection of plastic pots, there is a certain added sophistication that comes with growing your greenery in custom-made planters. Make just one for a prized specimen, or create a whole garden's worth. What's more, when frost threatens, you can move your garden indoors to enjoy during the colder months. (For heavy plants, you can even add wheels underneath the planter.)

This cylindrical planter brings to mind the old half-barrel planters while presenting a look that is both classic and up-to-date. Placing a plastic pot at its center keeps rot-causing soil and moisture away from the attractive woodwork. It can also save you from having to repot a new plant if it comes in a pot of the right size. The planter shown is made of white pine, painted to protect it from the elements. You can also use a weather-resistant wood such as cedar or redwood with a clear finish, or simply leave the planter to weather on its own. ❧

BUILDING THE PLANTER

The width of the slats is not a standard size, so you'll need to cut all these pieces to width—an operation best done with a table saw. If you don't have one, you may be able to have the cuts made at your lumberyard. As an alternative, use 1½-inch-wide strips (1 x 2s) and trim the last few strips to make things work out evenly. 🌺

HAVE ON HAND:

- ▶ Flowerpot
- ▶ Tape measure
- ▶ Saber saw or coping saw
- ▶ String and pencil
- ▶ Table saw
- ▶ Screw gun/drill and bits
- ▶ Primer and paint
- ▶ Paintbrush
- ▶ 1⅝-inch round/washer head screws

- ▶ ¾-inch AC plywood, 24 x 48-inch piece
- ▶ Eight 8-foot-long 1 x 3s

Cutting List:

- ▶ Two plywood disks: 21 inches in diameter
- ▶ Four spacers: 13⅝-inch-long 1 x 3s
- ▶ Thirty-six slats: ¾ x 1¹³/₁₆ x 18 inches

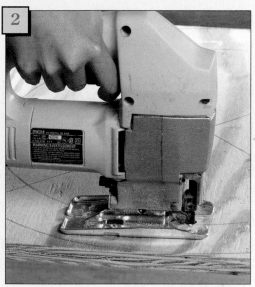

Lay out the disks (10½-inch radius) using a string and a pencil. The inner circles have radii of 8⁵/₁₆ and 4⅝ inches.

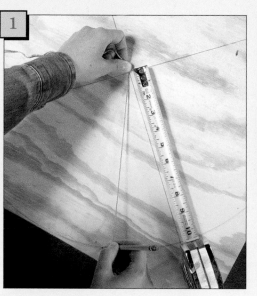

Cut the disks out with a saber saw. Start the inner cuts by drilling a hole through the plywood for the saw blade.

Using the miter gauge and a stop block, cut the spacers and the slats to the correct length on the table saw.

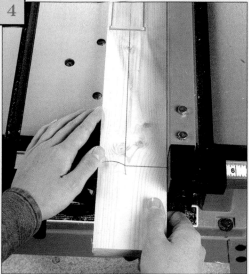

Rip the slats to a width of 1¹³/₁₆ inches. Leave two or three uncut for now to allow for error.

Prime and paint all surfaces on all the pieces. Painting both sides of everything will help keep the pieces from warping.

Screw the spacers at equal intervals in between the disks. Predrill the holes to keep the wood from splitting.

Predrill and screw the slats in place. The top of the slats should extend 2 inches beyond the top disk. Trim the last slats to fit.

Touch up the base coat of paint, then stencil or otherwise decorate the planter. Drop the pot in place, and you're ready to plant.

HERE'S HOW

A DIFFERENT-SIZED POT

If you would like to make a different-sized planter, get the plastic pot before you begin and build your planter to match. The diameter of the plywood disks should be 3 inches larger than that of the pot. You may also need to change the length of the support pieces and/or the width of the slats. Determining the slat width can be a little tricky. Measure the circumference of the plywood disks (roll them along a tape measure), then divide that number by 36. Cut the slats to this width, leaving three or four a little wide. Then, as you attach the slats, you can cut these three or four wider slats to account for any error.

Alternatives

INSTANT WATER FEATURES

Patio planters and half whiskey barrels make excellent containers for water gardens on decks or patios. Line the planter with a watertight container and add fish and some aquatic plants such as duckweed for a miniature oasis with a minimum of fuss. You can even leave enough space under the planter to house the pump and other mechanicals necessary for a small fountain, so you will be adding the sight and sound of running water to your garden as well.

You may discover that the sound of running water attracts birds to your garden. You could then view the planter as a base for a birdbath. With a small, thermostatically controlled heating element added to the pump, you can create an avian "spa" that will attract many different bird species year-round. If you decide to create a birdbath, there are a couple of things that you can do to make it even more attractive to these feathered creatures. If you are using a plastic container, you should be sure to scuff the surface with some coarse sandpaper to roughen it for traction. And you may want to add some rocks to serve as perches, so visitors can stop for a drink without getting their feet wet. 🌼

LEVELS OF PLANTERS

Planters don't necessarily have to be freestanding units. When built into the structure of a deck, they can add a sense of drama to the architecture while serving more everyday duties such as guardrail or bench end. The multi-tiered planter shown here does a great job of echoing the stairway next to it, calling attention to the change of levels. While the planter is essentially a simple square, the strong diagonal split into two triangles makes it seem much more complex. This makes for a nice combination—easy to build and practical, yet very attractive.

This planter was built from a variety of widths of 1-inch and 2-inch redwood and finished with an exterior transparent stain to maintain its rich, red color. The insides of the planter boxes are lined with plastic to keep moisture away from the wood. The plastic (and the box bottom) should have holes in them to promote good drainage. Ideally, you should use stainless steel fasteners to hold the pieces together, because regular, galvanized hardware will react with the redwood and leave dark streaks on the face of the boards. Predrill the holes for the screws, as redwood splits easily. 🌼

Three-Tiered Raised Bed

A multitiered raised bed overflowing with strawberries makes an attractive addition to your kitchen garden. And what's more, a fresh supply of berries right outside your kitchen door will enable you to make all kinds of favorite dishes, from jams to pies. Raised-bed gardening doesn't need to be limited to just strawberries. Any plant can benefit from this growing system. Having a raised bed allows you to provide just the right type of soil and drainage. And the raised growing surface makes the garden easier to tend as well.

You can build raised beds with a wide variety of materials, from stone and concrete to landscape timbers and even old truck tires. Most garden experts strongly advise against using pressure-treated or creosote-soaked lumber for raised beds, as the chemicals they contain may leach into the soil. Redwood and cedar are attractive choices, although even these naturally durable materials will rot fairly quickly when left in contact with the ground. The bed pictured is made from Trex with cedar trim. Trex (available at many home centers) is a man-made material composed of wood by-products and recycled plastic. Though somewhat more expensive than real wood, Trex lasts indefinitely outdoors. ❧

BUILDING THE BED

Y ou can cut Trex with the same saws and fasten it with the same screws and nails as for wood. For a raised bed of Trex, add extra support to the sides. ✿

HAVE ON HAND:

- ▶ Tape measure
- ▶ Circular saw
- ▶ Screw gun/drill
- ▶ Framing square
- ▶ Backsaw
- ▶ Miter box
- ▶ Level
- ▶ Hammer
- ▶ 3½-, 2½-, and 1⅝-inch screws
- ▶ Hardware cloth, ½-inch mesh
- ▶ Staple gun and fencing staples
- ▶ Spade and rake
- ▶ Three 12-foot-long pieces 2 x 6 Trex
- ▶ Seven 8-foot-long cedar 1 x 3s

Cutting List:

- ▶ Eight support blocks: 1½ x 2½ x 3-inch pieces of Trex
- ▶ Twenty cedar trim pieces: ¾ x 1⅞ x 26 inches

(remaining pieces are 2 x 6 Trex)

- ▶ Bottom: two 48-inch-long sides and two 45-inch-long sides
- ▶ Middle: two 34-inch-long sides and two 31-inch-long sides
- ▶ Top: two 24-inch-long sides and two 21-inch-long sides

Cut pieces for the frames to length. Screw corners together with 3½-inch deck screws. Check to make sure each frame is square.

Turn the frame assemblies over and staple hardware cloth to the undersides to protect plants from burrowing rodents.

Screw support blocks to the sides of the bottom and middle frames, centering them carefully. Blocks should be flush with the top of the sides.

Strip away the sod from the area for your new garden. Till the soil to a depth of 10 to 12 inches. Level the area with the back of a rake.

Set bottom frame in place; level it. Fill frame with a combination of topsoil and compost. Water thoroughly to settle the fill.

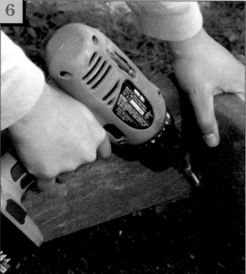

Place middle frame on bottom frame, with corners over support blocks; attach with two screws angled into each support block. Fill with soil mix.

Miter trim pieces to fit. On the sides of lower frames, the trim is made in two pieces to accommodate the corners of upper frames.

Place top frame as in Step 6, and fill with topsoil and compost mixture. Plant strawberries. Keep soil moist as plants become established.

HERE'S HOW
GROWING STRAWBERRIES

Many gardeners pinch the blossoms off their strawberry plants the first year, allowing the plants to put their energy into growing larger. In a raised-bed garden, you aren't all that interested in having the plants expand, so you can do just the opposite and then enjoy your first crop about 60 days after planting.

Choose everbearing plants (those that don't require specific periods of light and darkness) and plant them about 10 inches apart. Pinch off the runners as they start to grow, but leave the blossoms. Soon you'll be enjoying your first juicy crop.

Alternatives

LARGER-SCALE RAISED BEDS

By now, almost every gardener has heard about the benefits of gardening in raised beds: better drainage, easier weeding, faster soil warm-up in the spring, and so on. But taking the plunge and actually creating the beds is another matter—especially if you have been gardening on a flat plot for a while. Why? Well, building raised beds takes a fair amount of effort to begin with. However, if you are willing to put in the time, the results are well worth it.

Raised beds can be almost any size and shape. The sides for a raised bed can be made from a wide variety of materials, from various kinds of wood to concrete block to natural stone. You can even build a raised bed without any real structure simply by mounding up the soil in areas along access paths.

In this photo, the beds were made from pressure-treated landscape timbers spiked to the ground with lengths of steel reinforcing rod (rebar). Pressure-treated wood is acceptable for flower gardens, but you should use something else for vegetable gardens, as some of the preservative chemicals may leach into the soil. For the same reason, you should avoid using creosote-treated railroad ties. ❀

DRY-LAID STONE RAISED BED

Stone walls make excellent borders for raised beds. They are impervious to the elements, promote good drainage, and won't leach nasty chemicals into the soil. If your property has a lot of stone, you may have the materials for a beautiful raised bed right at hand. Or you can purchase stone from a masonry or landscape supplier.

Laying a stone wall is not as difficult as you might think, especially one that is only a foot or so tall. Start by laying out the outline of your intended bed on the ground with a rope or garden hose. Dig out the sod inside the rope or hose. Also dig down 12 inches around the perimeter where the stone will actually rest. Fill this shallow trench with ¾-inch gravel to promote drainage under the stones. Then start setting your stones in place.

Work your way up, stacking the stones on top of one another. Try to bridge the spaces between the stones in the courses below as you lay each successive course. Interlocking the stones this way makes for a stronger wall. Each stone you place should rest solidly on those below. If a stone wobbles, try it in a different position, or try a different stone. ❀

A Hinged Wall Trellis

Whether you grow flowering vines or edibles such as grapes, you'll find a trellis a useful addition to your garden. Build a freestanding one across the back of a garden to serve as a backdrop for your flower beds. Or incorporate one into a fence to add a splash of color along your boundaries. The trellis shown is mounted to an otherwise blank shed wall. Even before it is covered with vines, the trellis has a strong diagonal pattern that forms a pleasing visual counterpoint to the horizontal siding.

This project uses standard sizes of lumber—1 x 2s and 2 x 2s. If you want to leave the wood unfinished, use cedar or redwood, which is naturally decay resistant. If you are going to paint the trellis, any variety of wood will work. Be sure to use a good grade of paint and apply several coats—once the plants grow, you won't be able to paint again for a long time. The trellis is hinged, however, to allow you to paint the wall behind it. Simply undo the catches and fold the trellis down and out of the way. The trellis should be mounted several inches away from the side of a shed or a house to allow air to circulate, preventing mildew on the wall. ✿

MAKING THE TRELLIS

The trellis frame features half-lap joints at the corners. Once the frame is assembled, the slats fit inside. 🌾

HAVE ON HAND:

- ▶ Tape measure
- ▶ Circular saw
- ▶ Screw gun/drill
- ▶ Backsaw and miter box or power miter saw
- ▶ Hammer and nail set
- ▶ 1¼- and 2½-inch deck screws
- ▶ 4d finish nails
- ▶ Weather-resistant glue
- ▶ Wood putty
- ▶ Primer, paint, and paintbrush
- ▶ Two 2-inch T-hinges
- ▶ Two hook and eyes

- ▶ Four 8-foot-long 2 x 2s
- ▶ Ten 8-foot-long 1 x 2s

Cutting List:

- ▶ Two frame sides: 8-foot-long 2 x 2s
- ▶ Frame top and bottom: 36-inch-long 2 x 2s
- ▶ Center piece: 93-inch-long 2 x 2
- ▶ Thirty slats: 19-inch-long 1 x 2s
- ▶ Two verticals: ¾ x 1 x 91 inches
- ▶ Four mounting blocks: 6-inch-long 2 x 2s

Set the blade on your circular saw to cut halfway through the frame pieces for the lap joints. Make repeated cuts to remove the waste.

Join the corner joints with glue and 1¼-inch screws. Check to make sure the corners are square before the glue sets.

Cut the center piece to fit inside the frame. Center it, and then screw it in place with 2½-inch screws.

Cut the ends of the slats at a 60° angle. Check them against the frame to make sure the length is right.

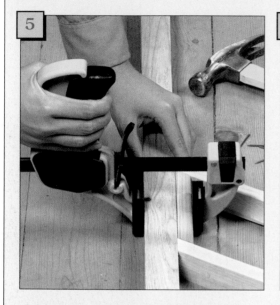

Cut a scrap piece of slat 5 inches long for a spacer. Clamp spacer to frame next to each slat as you nail the next slat in place.

Cut the top ends of the vertical pieces at 60°. Center them on the slats, drill pilot holes, and then glue and nail them in place.

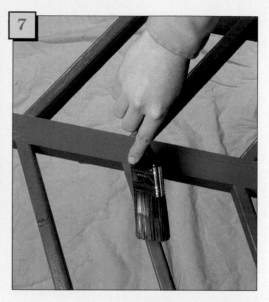

Fill the nail holes with exterior putty. Prime the trellis, then apply two coats of a high-quality exterior trim paint.

Screw the hinges to the trellis frame. Screw the first mounting block to siding. Screw in second block, 26 inches away from (and level with) first.

Prop the end of the trellis up on the mounting blocks and screw the hinges in place.

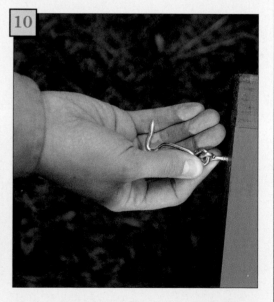

Tilt the trellis up into place. Attach the hooks to the top of the frame and screw the eyes into the side of the building.

Alternatives

PLANTS FOR A WALL TRELLIS

A wall trellis is the perfect stage for the vibrant flowers and foliage of climbing plants. But growing near a wall where sunlight can be intense and temperatures extreme can be a challenge for even the hardiest plants. Light-colored walls reflect sunlight, keeping themselves cool but increasing the intensity of the light on nearby foliage. Dark-colored walls absorb heat and can raise nearby air temperatures substantially. You can use color to modify the growing environment by painting south walls light colors and using darker tones on east, north, and west walls.

South-facing walls get a lot of sun and are often hot and bright. A south wall is a good place for tough plants, like trumpet creeper, or marginally hardy plants that appreciate a mild microclimate.

North walls are often shady and cold, with little direct sunlight. Climbing plants that may thrive on north walls include Virginia creeper and Boston ivy. Walls that face east or west are better for many plants. These exposures provide a few hours of warming sun each day coupled with some time in the shade. Many plants thrive in these conditions, including clematis, passionflower, Dutchman's pipe, five-leaved akebia, honeysuckle, jasmine, and mandevilla. ❧

CLEMATIS
Clematis 'Henryi'
8–10 feet tall
Zones 4–9
Vigorous climbing vine with large 4- to 6-inch-wide, creamy white flowers in summer; moist, well-drained soil enriched with compost; full sun; mulch to cool soil during growing season and prevent soil from heaving in winter.

PASSIONFLOWER
Passiflora spp.
12–20 feet tall
Zones 6–11
Fast-growing vine with green to maroon-green leaves and large, white, red, lavender, or violet flowers; evenly moist, average soil; full sun to partial shade; excellent container plant; produces 2- to 4-inch-long, green, yellow, orange, or purple fruit in warmer regions.

MANDEVILLA
Mandevilla spp.
10–20 feet tall
Zones 10–11
Tropical climbing vine with glossy, dark green leaves and large, tubular, pink to rose-colored flowers; consistently moist, well-drained soil; full sun with midday shade in warm climates; excellent container plant; blossoms attract hummingbirds.

TRUMPET CREEPER
Campsis radicans
20–30 feet tall
Zones 5–9
Very vigorous, woody vine with dark green leaves and brilliant, trumpet-shaped, scarlet flowers in summer to fall; needs strong support; prefers evenly moist, well-drained soil but tolerates poor soil; thrives in sun or shade but flowers best in full sun; blossoms attract hummingbirds.

HONEYSUCKLE
Lonicera sempervirens 'Sulphurea'
10–15 feet tall
Zones 5–9
Twining vine with thin, woody stems and dark greenish blue leaves; whorls of slender, sulfur-yellow, tubular flowers in summer followed by clusters of red berries in fall; blossoms attract hummingbirds; well-drained, moist soil; full sun to partial shade.

Erecting an Obelisk

Whether you use it to showcase a spectacular flowering vine or as a space-saving device for growing peas, this trellis in the form of an obelisk will grace your garden with a sense of elegance and style. Its gently tapering sides give it an architectural stance reminiscent of a city landscape, although it is perfectly at home against any garden backdrop. Top it with a gazing ball for an added effect.

Properly placed, the trellis can add a vertical presence to an otherwise low-lying bed. Plant a fast-growing annual vine at its feet, and you'll soon have a leafy backdrop for the other plants in the garden. When the weather turns colder, you can either store the trellis away for the winter or drape it with holiday lights for a festive look.

When you are building the trellis, predrill the holes for the screws that hold it together. This will help keep the wood from splitting as you drive the fasteners home. Also, even though the trellis does get painted, it is a good idea to use rust-proof screws. Regular screws will corrode quickly and leave rusty "tear" tracks down the trellis's legs. ❧

BUILDING THE TOWER

Build the tower one half at a time, then connect the two halves. Make the legs from pressure-treated wood, and the rest can be from ordinary pine. 🌸

HAVE ON HAND:

- ▶ Tape measure
- ▶ Circular saw
- ▶ Screw gun/drill and bits
- ▶ Sliding T-bevel
- ▶ 1⅝- and 3-inch deck screws
- ▶ Four 6-foot-long 2 x 2s, pressure treated
- ▶ Three 8-foot-long 1 x 2s
- ▶ Three 6-foot-long 1 x 4s
- ▶ Paint

Cutting List:

- ▶ Four legs: 6-foot-long 2 x 2s
- ▶ Two bottom rungs: 22⅝-inch-long 1 x 2s

- ▶ Two middle rungs: 18¼-inch-long 1 x 2s
- ▶ Two top rungs: 14¼-inch-long 1 x 2s
- ▶ Two bottom crossbars: 18⅛-inch-long 1 x 2s
- ▶ Two middle crossbars: 13¾-inch-long 1 x 2s
- ▶ Two top crossbars: 9¾-inch-long 1 x 2s
- ▶ Four long slats: ¾ x ¾ x 57¼ inches
- ▶ Eight short slats: ¾ x ¾ x 54 inches

Cut legs and rungs to length; screw together. Attach bottom rungs, 12 inches up; middle, 38½ inches up; top, 62½ inches up.

To strengthen the trellis, add a second screw to each joint. Be sure to predrill the holes to keep from splitting the wood.

The ends of the crossbars are cut to length at an 85° angle. Measure, then lay out these cuts with a sliding T-bevel.

To cut the crossbars, set a power miter saw to an 85° angle, or follow the layout lines with a circular saw.

5

Hold crossbars against rungs with their outer face in line with the inside faces of legs. Drill pilot holes and screw crossbars in place.

6

Cut the slats to size. Trim both ends of the short slats at an 85° angle.

7

Center three slats on each side of the trellis; screw them in place. The exact spacing is not critical but should be uniform on all sides.

8

Dig a 4-inch-deep hole for each leg. Set the tower in place, making sure it is standing up straight. Fill in the holes to anchor the tower.

HERE'S HOW

PAINTING THE TOWER

Even if you are painting with only one color, you may find it tough to coat all of the inside surfaces with the tower fully assembled. If this proves to be the case, you can always disassemble the two original sides from each other. Then paint all the pieces before reassembling.

Alternatives

A BAMBOO TOWER

Another way to create a vining tower is with lengths of bamboo, which are available from many garden centers. Bamboo is lightweight, weather resistant, and quite strong. For centuries, bamboo has been used for building in some parts of the world, but until recently, it has not been as common in this country.

Working with bamboo is a nice change of pace, especially if you are used to more conventional building materials such as framing lumber, nails, and screws. The only tools that you will need are a saw, a drill, and a pair of pliers. The process is quick and very easy to grasp. Galvanized wire is used to fasten the pieces together. To make a connection, hold the bamboo pieces together and mark them where they should be cut. Saw them to length, and hold them in place again. Drill through the pieces and feed a length of wire through the hole. Wrap the wire around the bamboo once or twice and twist the ends together to tighten the joint. Continue to add pieces this way until you are satisfied with your creation. If you are building a large structure, keep in mind that triangular forms are very strong. If your structure needs strengthening, try adding a diagonal brace or two. 🐾

A TRELLIS ADDS ROOM TO GROW

Vining structures don't have to be three-dimensional towers. The one shown here is essentially a flat panel tucked into a vegetable garden. Construction is very simple and straightforward. Sink two pressure-treated 2 x 2s into the ground at least 18 inches. Nail or screw a series of 1 x 2s between the uprights, alternating them front and back. Slide the diagonals and the center spire between the 1 x 2s and screw them in place. Paint the structure, then install some wires vertically between the horizontals, winding them around the 1 x 2s to keep them in place. These wires will give the vines something to cling to as they work their way skyward. As a final touch, add a fish or other whimsical garden figure to the top of the center spire to encourage your vines to prosper.

Such a vining structure adds a great deal of growing room to your garden without taking up much space. Try a crop of peas, runner beans, or even cucumbers, and you'll be delighted with how easy it is to harvest the bounty. Or plant a grapevine and start your own vineyard. (You may want to make the structure with some stronger materials to support a perennial vine.) 🐾

Constructing a Planter Bench

Equally at home on a deck or along a garden pathway, this planter bench provides a place to sit down and enjoy the beauty of the garden around you. The diagonal planters at either end keep you in close contact with the greenery and serve as anchors for the trestle-like bench. The planters are designed to hold standard plastic pots, which allows you to swap the pots in and out as different plants come into bloom. The plastic pots also keep the soil and moisture away from the wooden sides, so the planters should last a long time.

As shown, the planter bench is made from pine and spruce framing lumber and exterior plywood. It was given several coats of top-quality exterior enamel paint to protect it from the weather. You could also use cedar, redwood, or any other naturally weather-resistant wood and then leave the planter bench to weather naturally.

If you choose to set the planter bench directly on the ground, you should place a small pad of gravel underneath each end to help keep moisture away from the wood. Even with several coats of paint, wood that stays in direct contact with soil will soon begin to rot. 🌾

BUILDING THE BENCH

Get the plastic pots first and make the planters to fit them exactly, then make the bench to fit in between. ❧

HAVE ON HAND:

- ▶ Two plastic flowerpots
- ▶ Tape measure
- ▶ Circular saw
- ▶ Screw gun/drill
- ▶ 1⅝-inch round/washer head screws
- ▶ 1¼- and 3-inch deck screws
- ▶ Four 3½-inch bolts with washers and nuts
- ▶ ¾-inch 4x4-foot plywood
- ▶ Paint
- ▶ Three 8-foot-long 1x3s
- ▶ Eight 8-foot-long 1x6s
- ▶ Two 8-foot-long 2x4s

- ▶ 10-foot-long 2x6
- ▶ 8-foot-long 2x6

Cutting List:

- ▶ Four plywood squares: 18½ x 18½ inches
- ▶ Eight corner slats: ¾ x 2⅛ x 20 inches
- ▶ Thirty-two side slats: ¾ x 3⅞ x 20 inches
- ▶ Four braces: ¾ x 2 x 22 inches
- ▶ Two stretchers: 65-inch-long 2x4s
- ▶ Three crosspieces: 11⅛-inch-long 2x4s
- ▶ Seat: two 64-inch and one 52-inch-long 2x6s

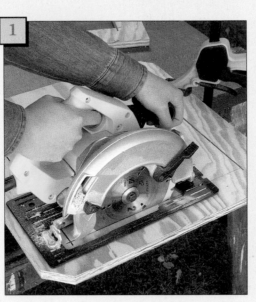

Cut top and bottom squares to size. Cut a 13½-inch square from center of tops. Measure 1½ inches from each corner; cut as shown.

Cut corner slats to size. Screw them to tops and bottoms, with the bottom ¾ inch up from end of slats, and the top 17¼ inches up.

Sand the corners of the side slats to create a shadow line, then screw them to the top and bottom squares, even with the corner slats.

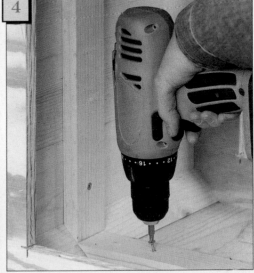

Cut corners off braces so they fit inside planters. Screw them in place to the sides of the planters where the bench will attach.

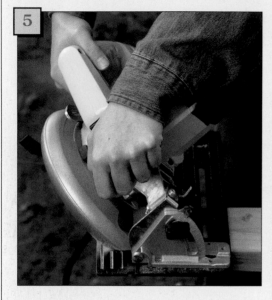

5

Tilt the blade on your circular saw to 45°; cut stretchers to length. The length of the longer side of the stretcher should be 65 inches.

6

Cut crosspieces to length; screw them in place between the stretchers. Center one and locate the others 12 inches in from the ends.

7

Have a helper hold stretchers against planters. Top should be 14½ inches high. Screw stretchers in place temporarily from inside.

8

Drill a 1-inch counterbore into each stretcher at an angle, holding drill perpendicular to side of planter. Finish hole with ⅜-inch bit. Bolt in place.

9

Cut seat boards to length. The ends of long pieces are cut at 45°. Screw seat boards to stretchers.

10

Paint planter to suit your décor. Then go to your local garden center and choose some lovely plants to inhabit your new planter bench.

Alternatives

LET THE WOOD SHINE THROUGH

You may prefer furniture with a clear finish that allows the natural beauty of the wood to show through. Redwood and cedar are excellent woods for such pieces and hold up well outdoors. They aren't your only choices, however. Teak, mahogany, cypress, and even oak will make good-looking, long-lasting outdoor furniture and accents as well. Keep in mind that all these woods will eventually turn gray if left unprotected. To maintain the wood's original color, you'll have to apply a protective finish such as spar varnish and renew it periodically.

The planter bench shown here is made of redwood and was treated with a penetrating outdoor finish that provides protection and a slight sheen. The finish should be reapplied annually to maintain the bench's appearance. Construction of the bench is fairly simple. Start by making the frames that hold the planters together. Screw the pieces together and plug the holes. Then add the vertical pieces that make up the sides. Finally, put together the slats that make up the seat. Note that all the corners on the pieces have been rounded over with a router for a smooth appearance. ❧

AGING GRACEFULLY

There is a certain feeling of accomplishment that you get when the last coat of paint is dry and you finally set your latest project in place out in the garden. But it does not take long before sunlight, wind, and rain begin to take their toll and that beautiful project doesn't look as new as it once did. There are a couple of approaches you can take when this happens. The first is the one practiced by the U.S. Navy and the folks at Disney World—paint, paint, and repaint, just as soon as anything shows signs of weathering (and sometimes before). This isn't a bad policy, especially for things like houses and sheds, which really need good protection from the elements. But it may be overkill for the smaller items in your garden.

A second, more relaxed approach is to allow your projects to age for a while before refurbishing them. To a certain extent, the scrapes and dings that come from use, as well as a little peeled paint here and there, can add character to your garden accents and make them that much more attractive. Plus, by putting off repainting for a while, you'll have more time to enjoy your garden and maybe even make some more projects. ❧

Making a Plant Stand

Potted plants are a great way to keep the joy of gardening going year-round. Outside on the deck during the summer, they bring your garden a little closer to your home and punctuate the area with their colorful foliage and blooms. Inside your house, during the colder winter months, they can brighten rooms and serve as a reminder of better weather to come.

Finding a good way to display your potted friends can be something of a challenge. Instead of resorting to a series of shelves cobbled together from cement blocks and boards, why not try your hand at building this simple little stand? Its light, colorful design fits in with almost any décor as it sets off the beauty of your portable garden. With its painted finish, it is at home both indoors and out and cleans up easily after the inevitable spills and messes.

This particular stand was designed to hold a small, intimate menagerie of plants—maybe six or eight pots worth—with smaller pots on the top shelf and larger ones below. If you have a bigger collection, you can easily expand the stand by building two bases, then cutting some longer shelves to go in between them. ❧

BUILDING THE STAND

I t is easier to make the angled rip cuts here with a table saw. You can use a circular saw for those cuts by tilting its blade and using an edge guide. ❀

HAVE ON HAND:

- Tape measure
- Square
- Circular saw
- Hammer
- Saber saw
- Screw gun/drill and bits
- String and pencil
- 6d finish nails
- 1⅝- and 3-inch screws
- Wood putty
- Paint
- 8-foot-long 1 x 4
- 8-foot-long 1 x 6
- ¾-inch AC plywood, 2 x 4 feet

Cutting List:
- Upright: 31-inch-long 1 x 4
- Narrow upright: ¾ x 2¾ x 31 inches
- Front legs: 9¼-inch-long 1 x 6s
- Two front supports: ¾ x 2½ x 6 inches
- Back leg: 31-inch-long 1 x 6
- Back support: ¾ x 2½ x 17 inches
- Back: 5 x 22½-inch plywood
- Shelves: 13 x 36-inch and 9 x 18-inch plywood

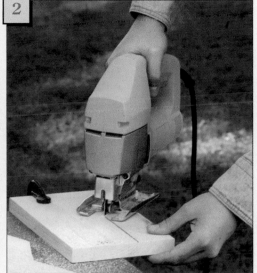

Cut uprights to length. Tilt circular saw blade to 45°; rip uprights to width, beveling one side. Nail pieces together to form a right angle.

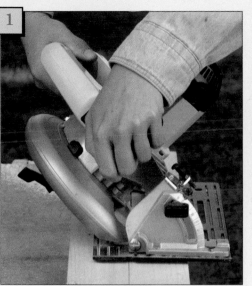

Cut the front legs to size, then lay out the foot profile on each. Cut the legs to shape with a saber saw.

Screw one front leg to each upright, centering them. The upper edge of legs should be 5½ inches from the end of each upright.

Cut front shelf supports to size; taper them from ¼ inch at one end to 2½ inches at the other. Screw them to the uprights even with the top end.

HERE'S HOW

AN IMPERVIOUS SURFACE

Painting the shelves on the plant stand will protect them from spills for a long time. Eventually, however, you'll need to repaint. As an alternative, you might want to consider facing the shelves with plastic laminate, the same stuff kitchen counters are made of. Plastic laminate is practically indestructible and will last indefinitely, even if you have toddlers helping you to garden. It is available in a wide variety of colors from your local building center. Use contact cement to stick it in place.

Cut ends of back leg and support to match front legs and supports. Screw pieces to the upright, centering them from end to end.

Cut the back to fit in between the back support and the back leg. Screw it in place to the upright.

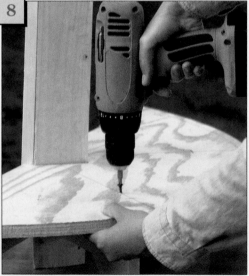

Mark the top shelf radius at 9 inches; mark the bottom shelf at 19 inches, with a center point 6 inches from edge. Make cuts with a saber saw.

Cut bottom shelf to fit around the upright. Place shelves on the stand and screw them in place. Paint the stand to suit your taste.

Alternatives

PLANTS FOR PLANT STANDS

A plant stand is a versatile portable garden that you can change as often as you like or move to other locations for entertaining or to add ambiance. A stand makes an attractive accent for the deck or patio during the warmer months, and it can be moved indoors during winter, when a display of plants is especially welcome.

Decorating a plant stand can be as much fun as enjoying the finished display. In many ways, decorating a plant stand is like getting a free wish from the garden genie, because the end result can match any mood or style you choose.

When deciding what plants to use on a plant stand, let your imagination run a little wild. Pots of annuals such as petunias and marigolds offer a rainbow of bright colors, are easy to care for, and bloom for weeks on end. Pots of vining plants like sweet potato and nasturtium create a flowing display that cascades from level to level, top to bottom.

Perennials offer a wide range of colors and flower forms to please the most discriminating gardener. For a neat and tidy display try containers of low mounding plants such as 'Mount Spokane' violet or 'Miss Muffet' Shasta daisy. You can create a tropical look with pots of large-flowered yellow and red daylilies intermingled with containers of red, yellow, or orange Hawaiian hibiscus. 🌸

DAYLILY
Hemerocallis spp.
2–6 feet tall
Zones 3–11
Clump-forming, deciduous, evergreen, or semi-evergreen perennial with long, slender leaves; large, white, yellow, pink, apricot, or red blossoms in summer; divide clumps every 3 to 5 years to maintain vigor; moist, well-drained soil; full sun to partial shade; tolerates poor soil and drought.

HAWAIIAN HIBISCUS
Hibiscus rosa-sinensis
3–15 feet tall
Zones 10–11
Popular tropical shrub with dark green, shiny leaves on woody stems; flowers are large, up to 6 inches wide, in colors including white, yellow, orange, and red; moist, well-drained, fertile soil; fertilize monthly during the growing season; full sun; excellent container plant.

VIOLET
Viola 'Mount Spokane'
6–8 inches tall
Zones 5–10
Delicate clumps of medium green foliage beneath abundant, pure white flowers edged in pale blue; blossoms appear continuously from late spring to fall and are lightly fragrant; moist, fertile soil; full sun to partial shade.

SHASTA DAISY
Leucanthemum x *superbum* 'Miss Muffet'
10–15 inches tall
Zones 5–9
Clump-forming perennial with rosette of dark green, sharply lobed leaves; blossoms have abundant, white, ray flowers surrounding a bright yellow, central disk; well-drained, evenly moist, fertile soil; full sun to light shade; flowers attract beneficial insects and butterflies.

PETUNIA
Petunia spp.
6–18 inches tall
Annual
Large group of upright to creeping annuals with medium green, slightly sticky leaves and small to large, bell-shaped flowers in a range of colors including white, yellow, red, blue, purple, and bicolors. Prefers rich, well-drained, consistently moist soil; full sun.

Attracting Wildlife
to Your Garden

There are many ways a garden can help keep you in tune with the natural world and its changes of season. You can delight in the first bulbs pushing their way intrepidly through the snow, and marvel at the colors of the autumn foliage blazing against the sky. With very little added effort, you can also bring other vanguards of the coming months into your own private Eden by making your garden a friendly place for migrating birds to visit.

It doesn't take much to attract a wide variety of birds to your yard. Provide a few simple necessities, such as food, shelter, and water, and you'll soon have an ongoing show outside your windows that will entertain you for hours. You will likely discover how easy it is to get hooked on the joys of bird watching. You may even find yourself keeping track of when each species appears during a certain season and making lists of the different varieties you manage to attract. By building some or all of the projects in this section, you can dramatically increase your chances of adding new birds to your life list. At the same time you'll be providing a valuable service to our feathered friends. ❧

Building a Bluebird House

The story of the eastern bluebird's return is a bright spot in our often bleak environmental record. By establishing bluebird "trails" of nesting boxes, birders and other conservationists have reestablished these bright, cheery creatures in the wild landscape east of the Rocky Mountains. You can join this effort by building and maintaining a bluebird house of your own. (Though the eastern bluebird gets more attention, western bluebirds would also enjoy one of these houses.)

This is a great project to get children interested in both gardening and ecology. The house can be built quickly and easily on a winter weekend morning. Then, once the weather begins to turn warmer, you can make an expedition to find the perfect location. Eastern bluebirds prefer houses at the verge where forest and field meet, while western bluebirds seem to prefer ponderosa pine forests. Once the house is placed, sit back and enjoy as your young naturalist watches "her" bluebirds raise a family and consume large quantities of insects. At season's end, you can open the box to clean it out for next year. You'll be amazed at all the different materials these avian architects weave into their homes.

MAKING THE HOUSE

This design has several bird-friendly features: Drain holes and a wire-mesh platform keep the nest clean; double-thick wood at the entry stops predators; and roof overhangs help keep rain out. Almost any wood will work here, but don't use pressure-treated wood, as it isn't good for the birds. ❧

HAVE ON HAND:

- ▶ Tape measure
- ▶ Circular saw (or table saw)
- ▶ Bevel gauge
- ▶ Screw gun/drill and bits
- ▶ 1½-inch drill bit
- ▶ 1⅝-inch weatherproof screws
- ▶ ½-inch mesh hardware cloth, 5 x 7-inch piece
- ▶ Brass L-hook
- ▶ 6-foot-long 1 x 10 cedar board

Cutting List:
- ▶ Back: ¾ x 6½ x 14 inches
- ▶ Two sides: ¾ x 5¾ x 11⅝ inches
- ▶ Bottom: ¾ x 5 x 5 inches
- ▶ Front: ¾ x 5 x 9⅝ inches
- ▶ Roof: ¾ x 8½ x 9 inches
- ▶ Entry: ¾ x 2½ x 3¼ inches

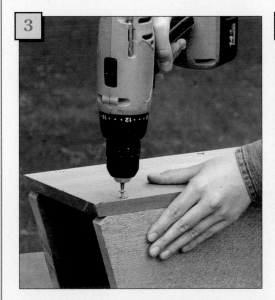

Cut all the pieces to size. When cutting the sides, mark the angle from back to front at approximately 71°. Cut along lines with a circular saw.

So that back top edge aligns with sides, tilt your saw blade to match their angle. Trim (bevel) one end of the back at this angle.

Cut the upper corners off the sides as shown, then screw them to the back. Align the bevel on the back with the angle of the sides.

Cut the corners off the bottom as shown. Drill a series of ⅜-inch holes in a circular pattern all the way through the piece for drainage.

Slip the bottom piece in place between the sides. Attach it with one screw through each side and one through the back.

Bevel the edges of the entry and screw it to the front, ½ inch down from the top. Drill a 1½-inch entry hole through both pieces.

Attach the front with one screw driven through each side near the top. The front should pivot on these screws for cleaning.

Screw the roof in place so it overhangs the back by ¾ inch. Check to be sure entry clears roof when you open front.

Bend the hardware cloth to make a platform and insert it into the house. Screw an L-hook at the bottom center of the front to keep it shut.

Screw the house to a post in a grassy area away from shrubs and trees. The entry hole should be 5 to 10 feet off the ground.

Alternatives

BIRDS OF A DIFFERENT FEATHER

Bluebirds aren't the only birds that live in houses. The basic design shown on page 60 works well for attracting many different species, though you may need to change the size of the entry hole or the size of the house. Then, when you are placing the house, consider where the bird you are hoping to attract prefers to live. Some, like bluebirds and tree swallows, like open areas. Others, like woodpeckers, prefer to be higher in the trees of a forested site.

Here are a few of the many birds you may be able to host and their preferred accommodations and locations (all these houses should be 8 to 10 inches deep):

Nuthatches: entry hole 1¼ inches, interior 4 x 4 inches; woodland

Chickadees: entry hole 1⅛ inches, interior 4 x 4 inches; brushy borders

Flycatchers: entry hole 2 inches, interior 6 x 6 inches; forest edges

Titmice: entry hole 1¼ inches, interior 4 x 4 inches; woodland

Downy woodpeckers: entry hole 1¼ inches, interior 4 x 4 inches; open woodland ✺

SQUIRREL DETERRENCE

Birds aren't the only creatures that will be anxious to move into your newly made dwelling. Mice, squirrels, and even wasps may take up residence. None of these make particularly good tenants. Wasps are probably the most difficult to deal with—you won't want to use an insecticide, because the spray is also harmful to birds. A high-pressure blast of water from a hose is sometimes effective—just be ready to run when the wasps come flying out to see what is going on.

There are several things you can try to defeat rodents. A baffle attached to the post may deter mice from making the climb. But squirrels may prove to be more persistent. What's worse, they like to remodel, often gnawing away at the entry hole to make it more squirrel-sized. Deal with this the same way you would deal with human vandals—get a stronger door. Most hardware stores sell aluminum bar stock that is ⅛ inch thick and 1½ inches or so wide. Purchase a length of this and cut two pieces about 4 inches long. File half an entry hole in each piece as shown, then drill and countersink these pieces for screws. Screw the metal pieces over the entryway to frustrate all but the toughest squirrels. ✺

Constructing a Wren House

In addition to providing a cozy home for some of your wild friends, building birdhouses has other benefits. A resident family of house wrens can provide hours of entertainment as you watch and listen to your new neighbors setting up housekeeping. You may even be inspired to get on with some of the chores you've been putting off when you see how busy a pair of wrens can be—especially once they have little ones to feed. And imagine the swell of pride you'll feel when your first "family" fledges and sets out on its own.

Your new tenants won't be freeloaders, either. Birds consume an amazing amount of food for their size. With migrating, reproducing, and simply staying warm to contend with, the average bird consumes many times its own weight each year just to survive. Depending on the species, this can mean fewer insects, weed seeds, even rodents (no, wrens don't eat mice—just their food supply) to deal with, without resorting to more drastic and environmentally harmful measures. So build a few wren houses or houses for other species, and sit back and enjoy the show. 🐾

BUILDING THE HOUSE

This wren house is fairly straightforward to put together. Having access to a table saw will make the angled cuts easier. The house's most unusual feature is the tin roof. It is made from part of a #10 food can, cut and fit to the top of the house. Choose a light color to paint the roof to avoid having your wren house become a little solar oven. 🌼

HAVE ON HAND:

- ▶ Tape measure
- ▶ T-bevel
- ▶ Protractor
- ▶ Saber saw
- ▶ Table saw
- ▶ Screw gun/drill and bits
- ▶ Aviator's snips
- ▶ Hammer
- ▶ 4-foot-long 1 x 8
- ▶ 2-pound coffee can (with ends removed)

- ▶ 2-inch screws
- ▶ ¾-inch nails
- ▶ Paintbrush and paint
- ▶ Eyebolts

Cutting List:

- ▶ Two front/back pieces: ¾ x 6 x 6¾ inches
- ▶ Two sides: ¾ x 3⁵⁄₁₆ x 4 inches
- ▶ Bottom: ¾ x 4¼ x 4 inches

Cut front and back to size. Use a protractor and a T-bevel to lay out 75° side angles. Cut along layout lines with a saber saw.

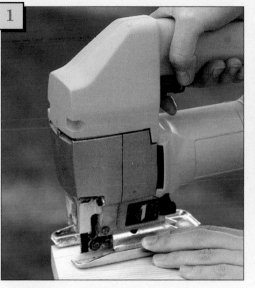

Trace around the can to lay out the curved cut on the front and back. Make the cut with your saber saw.

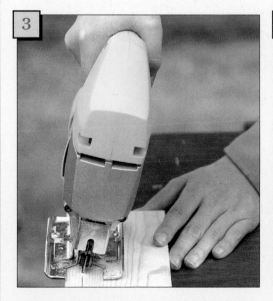

Cut a piece of wood for the sides slightly longer than you need. Rip it to width with the saw blade tilted to 75°. Cut sides to length.

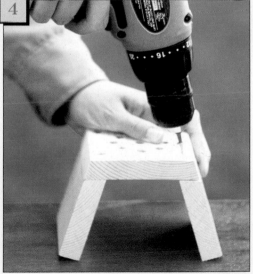

Cut bottom to size, beveling both side edges at 75°. Drill a series of ⅜-inch holes in bottom for drainage. Screw bottom to sides.

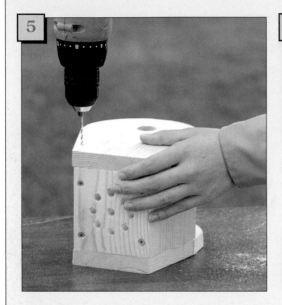

Drill a 1-inch hole in the center front, 1¾ inches down from top of curve. Screw front and back to side/bottom assembly.

Mark two lines on can, dividing it in half. Make third line, 1½ inches from second. Cut can along first and third lines. Use larger piece for roof.

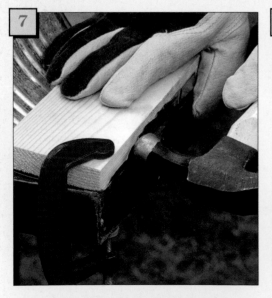

Trim ⅜ inch off the rim from the four corners of the can. Hammer the resulting flap over to eliminate the sharp edge.

Paint roof and house as desired. Attach eyebolts to roof for hanging. Nail roof to house, with most of the overhang over the hole.

HERE'S HOW

HANGING THE HOUSE

You can hang your wren house in a tree, support it on a pipe, or even attach it to the side of a building or post. To hang the house from a branch, purchase some eyebolts and drill holes for them through the roof. For pipe mounting, purchase an 8-foot length of steel water pipe and a floor flange. Drive the pipe into the ground, then thread the flange on the end of the pipe. Screw the house to the flange. To mount the house on the side of a post or building, simply drive screws through the back of the house.

Alternatives

A BAT HOUSE

One more flying creature you'll be happy to host is the bat. Despite all the scary stories associated with these furry flying mammals, the benefits of having them around far outweigh the heebie-jeebies they may cause. Consider that just one bat can consume up to 500 mosquitoes an hour, and that they are active when most insect-eating birds have called it quits for the day. Suddenly playing landlord to a bat colony doesn't sound all that bad. Bats are also valuable as pollinators, helping to propagate many different species of vegetation.

Bats thrive in colonies, so a bat house should be big enough for 20 or 30 animals. The one shown is roughly 20 inches tall, 10 inches wide, and 3 inches deep. It is open at the bottom and has a series of shallow saw cuts across the inside of the front to give the bats a place to hold on to. You could make a larger version with one or more vertical dividers inside to house a larger colony.

The best place to install a bat house is under the eaves of your house. This will help keep the bats safe from predators. Positioning the house to receive a little morning sunlight also seems to encourage bats to take up residence. ❦

A NESTING PLATFORM

There are a number of bird species that prefer an open shelter in which to nest. These include robins, barn swallows, phoebes, and song sparrows. You can easily accommodate birds such as these by building a simple nesting platform like the one shown. It features a shelf that is open on three sides and a roof to help provide a little shelter for the nest underneath.

The platform should be mounted high enough off the ground to provide protection from cats and other predators. Under the eaves of a house or outbuilding or on a window ledge is an ideal place, as the building's roof overhang provides more shelter from the elements. You can also hang the platform on the downwind side of a tree.

Robins, in particular, are fun birds to attract. These cheery harbingers of spring are quite tolerant of humans and will raise a family right in the middle of a busy garden. They often raise two broods of young in a season, but they seem to prefer to relocate to a new nest after each brood. So you may find that once the first bunch fledges and is on its way, you can attract a second family of robins by removing the original nest and cleaning the platform up a bit. ❦

A Versatile Ground Feeder

Birds make fine garden companions. A little shelter, food, and water are all they ask for in return for hours of entertainment on cold winter days. To attract the widest possible variety of birds to your feeding stations, it pays to have a number of different types of feeders. Some birds, such as finches, titmice, and chickadees, come readily to traditional, pole-mounted feeders (see page 72 for a potential design). Others, such as juncos, mourning doves, and cardinals, prefer to feed at or near ground level.

Although you could just spread some seed on a tray left on the ground, the tray will quickly collect water, and the treats you offer your feathered friends will rot. This feeder design overcomes that problem. Its short legs keep the seed away from direct ground contact, and the screen bottom allows rainwater to flow right through. Upkeep of the feeder is relatively minimal. Fill it with fresh seed every day or so (more often in very cold weather). Before you dump in the new seed, remove the empty shells that have accumulated. Once the birds discover this low-lying buffet, you'll be amazed at the variety this simple feeder will attract. 🦚

BUILDING THE FEEDER

Make your feeder from a rot-resistant wood such as redwood or cedar. If the feeder attracts other wildlife such as deer, put a wire cage on top to keep larger critters at bay. 🌺

HAVE ON HAND:

- ► Tape measure
- ► Circular saw
- ► Screw gun/drill and bits
- ► Miter box
- ► Backsaw
- ► Clamp
- ► Weather-resistant glue
- ► 1¼- and 1⅝-inch deck screws
- ► Window screen
- ► Hardware cloth, ½-inch mesh
- ► Wire snips
- ► Staple gun and staples

- ► Sandpaper
- ► Birdseed
- ► 6-foot-long cedar 1 x 4

Cutting List:

- ► Two long sides: ¾ x 1½ x 20 inches
- ► Two short sides: ¾ x 1½ x 11½ inches
- ► Two long strips: ½ x ¾ x 20 inches
- ► Two short strips: ½ x ¾ x 11½ inches
- ► Four legs: ¾ x 2½ x 4 inches

Cut the frame pieces to size and screw them together with 1⅝-inch deck screws. Predrill holes to prevent wood from splitting.

Clamp a miter box to your workbench. Use it as a guide as you cut the ends of the corner braces off at a 45° angle.

Predrill screw holes, then glue and screw the braces in place with a weather-resistant glue and 1¼-inch deck screws.

Cut the window screen and hardware cloth to size, using the frame as a pattern. Staple both pieces to the underside of the frame.

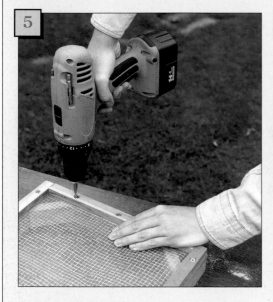

Reinforce the screens at the edges with four strips. Predrill the strips and screw them in place with 1¼-inch screws.

Cut the legs to the shape shown (the exact dimensions and angle are not critical). Smooth the sawn edges with sandpaper.

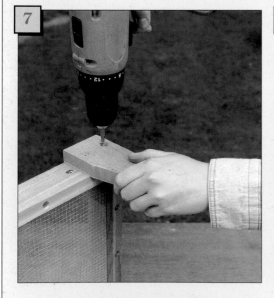

Predrill the legs for screws, then screw them to the sides of the feeder with 1¼-inch screws.

Place the feeder in your garden and cover the screen with a birdseed mixture, then settle back and wait for the show.

HERE'S HOW

ATTRACTING BIRDS

Along with providing food, there are a couple of other things you can do to make your garden more bird-friendly. First, provide some water (preferably ice-free). A birdbath or a small pond will do the trick. Birds seem to be particularly attracted to the sound of running water, so you might want to add a small pump to circulate the water. And second, place your feeders near (4 to 6 feet away) but not too close to some sheltering foliage. The birds will appreciate the cover, but you don't want to give the neighborhood cats a place to arrange an ambush.

Alternatives

SEEDS TO ATTRACT WILD BIRDS

To get the most enjoyment from feeding wild birds be sure to provide your feathered friends with the correct type of seed. Many species of birds have strong preferences for a certain type of food.

The type of wild bird food preferred by the greatest number of birds is black oil sunflower seed. These small, dark-colored seeds provide excellent nutrition and have a high oil content to help keep birds warm in winter. Black-striped sunflower seed is nearly as popular. Both of these seeds can be used in ground and hanging feeders.

White proso millet is an inexpensive feed that is very attractive to small, ground-feeding birds such as juncos and sparrows, and larger birds including doves and jays.

Very large birds, such as wild turkeys, are attracted to whole-kernel corn and cracked corn. Doves also will eat corn, but doves are notorious for not being very picky about what they eat for dinner. Mix a little turkey grit in with the seed to help the birds digest their food better.

When the weather turns very cold, a mixture of feed with a high oil content, such as peanut kernels and black oil sunflower seeds, will help birds stay warm. Avoid using peanut hearts, as many birds will not eat them. 🐦

AMERICAN TREE SPARROW
Spizella arborea
6 inches long
Song: teedle-weet
A common winter resident across much of United States and southern Canada from the Maritimes south to the Carolinas and west to the mountains of the Pacific Coast. Habitat includes fields, brushy scrub, residential areas, and marshes.

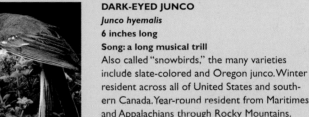

DARK-EYED JUNCO
Junco hyemalis
6 inches long
Song: a long musical trill
Also called "snowbirds," the many varieties include slate-colored and Oregon junco. Winter resident across all of United States and southern Canada. Year-round resident from Maritimes and Appalachians through Rocky Mountains. Habitat includes suburbs and forest edges.

BLUE JAY
Cyanocitta cristata
11 inches long
Song: a rolling toodle-oodle
Noisy, bossy birds resident from Maritimes west across southern Canada to Great Plains and south to Texas and Florida. Habitat is extremely varied, from suburban yards to forests, fields, wetlands, and towns. Population and range expanding into Rocky Mountain region.

MOURNING DOVE
Zenaida macroura
12 inches long
Song: who-ahh-who-who-who
Resident across most of United States, from central New England to Florida and west to Pacific Coast. Extends range in summer to include northern tier of states from Rocky Mountains to Maritime Canada. Habitat includes open fields, farmland, residential areas, and forest edges.

WILD TURKEY
Meleagris gallopavo
48 inches long
Song: gobble-gobble-gobble
Very large birds related to domestic turkeys. Resident populations in all lower 48 states and parts of southern Canada. Habitat includes open forests, forest edges, swamps, and rural backyards. Population and range expanding. Visits ground feeders in flocks of 6 to 30 birds.

Building a Bird Feeder

If you want to attract birds to your garden, nothing does the job like a feeding station or two. Keep your feeder filled year-round, and you'll have a constant, ever-changing parade of visitors to keep you entertained. It's fun to keep track of the various species that drop by and the approximate dates they show up. Compare your lists from year to year, and you'll begin to get a feel for when certain birds are on the move during their seasonal migration.

This feeder has some features that make it easy to maintain. First, it is built of cedar, so it will last a long time out in the elements without rotting. Its copper roof adds durability and a bit of rich texture to the landscape. The seed tray has a mesh bottom for good drainage, which keeps the feed from going bad. And the hopper holds a lot of seed, so you won't have to fill it very often (depending on the size of your visitors' appetites, of course).

Place the feeder where you can see it easily from inside. Try to keep it about 5 feet away from shrubs or other cover that might give the neighborhood cats the upper hand when stalking your feathered friends. ❧

BUILDING THE FEEDER

The feeder is easily built with common tools. The work will go a little faster with a table saw. If you have trouble finding copper, try a roofing supplier. ❧

HAVE ON HAND:

- ▶ Tape measure
- ▶ Circular saw
- ▶ Protractor
- ▶ Screw gun/drill and bits
- ▶ Tin snips
- ▶ Hammer
- ▶ 1¼- and 2-inch deck screws
- ▶ Screen
- ▶ Hardware cloth, ½-inch mesh
- ▶ Staple gun
- ▶ 1¼-inch piano hinge
- ▶ 9 x 10-inch copper, 18 gauge
- ▶ ⅝-inch copper nails

- ▶ ⅛-inch-thick acrylic plastic, 5⅜ x 21⅜ inches
- ▶ 8-foot-long cedar 1 x 6

Cutting List:
- ▶ Back: ¾ x 5 x 23½ inches
- ▶ Two sides: 24-inch-long 1 x 6s
- ▶ Narrow roof: ¾ x 2 x 9 inches
- ▶ Wide roof: 9-inch-long 1 x 6
- ▶ Two perch frame sides: ¾ x ⅞ x 5 inches
- ▶ Perch frame front: ¾ x ⅞ x 8⅛ inches

Cut back and sides to length. Then cut the sides so they taper from 5½ inches wide at the top to 2½ inches wide at the bottom.

Cut across tops of the sides at a 67° angle, and across bottoms at 78°. Tilt saw blade, and bevel ends of back to match.

Set saw for a shallow (about ¼-inch) cut. Cut grooves for acrylic front window in sides. Locate grooves ¼ inch in from front edges.

Screw sides to back. Hinge the two roof pieces together. Attach roof by driving two screws through the smaller piece into the sides.

Cut perch frame pieces. (Leave front long; you can trim it later.) Screw perch frame sides to feeder and perch frame front to frame sides.

Cut the screen and hardware cloth to match the perch frame. Staple them to the underside of the feeder with the screen against the frame.

Cut two pieces of copper to overhang the roof by ¼ inch. Trim corners, then hammer copper to fit. Attach with copper nails.

Drive two screws through back to hang it. Cut a ½-inch notch in bottom of plastic front so seed can fall through; slide front into place.

HERE'S HOW

WORKING WITH PLASTIC

You can get the plastic used for the front of the feeder at most places that sell replacement glass for windows. Either acrylic plastic (Plexiglas) or polycarbonate plastic (Lexan) will work well. Both of these plastics are easily cut with regular woodworking tools and equipment.

When you are ready to cut the notch in the front for the seed opening, lay out the opening on the paper that comes with the plastic. Cut out the notch with a coping saw. Peel away the paper to expose the plastic.

Alternatives

A SPECIAL FEEDER FOR BLUEBIRDS

A regular bird feeder will attract all sorts of birds, depending on which area of the country you live in. But you probably will never see a bluebird dining there. That is because bluebirds mainly eat insects, and not the seeds usually found in bird feeders. While some of the bird catalogs sell special "bluebird" food, it has limited appeal to these brightly colored creatures because it doesn't crawl around. If you want to improve your chances of attracting bluebirds to your feeding stations, you have to put an entrée on the menu that you can be certain they'll like: mealworms, available at any pet store.

The feeder shown here is designed especially for feeding bluebirds. It features two entry holes—irresistible to these cavity-dwelling birds—and a large window so you can see them enjoying their meal. By offering the mealworms in an enclosed place, you can have some control over which birds you are feeding. This also helps to keep the main course from wandering away before the bluebirds arrive. Mix in some raisins, peanut suet, and even cornmeal (key ingredients in commercial bluebird mixes) to round out the menu. ❦

WOODPECKER FEEDER

Other birds you can attract to your feeders include woodpeckers—provided you offer the right kind of food. Woodpeckers are similar to bluebirds in that they prefer a diet of insects. (That's usually what they are after when drumming their bills on your house in the still wee hours of a Sunday morning.) Unlike bluebirds, however, you can usually get woodpeckers to stop by for a treat of peanut suet, or even peanut butter. Both these foods are messy, so you'll probably want to set up a separate feeder for them to help keep your other feeders cleaner.

This feeder is designed to present woodpeckers with a treat in a manner with which they are familiar—lodged in a section of a tree. To build the feeder, find a piece of a tree and bore a series of holes along its length. You can add some perches if you wish (though the woodpeckers don't seem to particularly need them) and a roof, mainly to make the feeder more attractive. Hang the feeder on a tree where you can see it from your favorite observation point. Fill the holes with a mix of peanut suet and peanut butter, and you'll soon have a regular parade of woodpeckers visiting your garden. ❦

Casting a Birdbath

Along with food and nesting boxes, an optimal bird garden also provides water for its winged guests. This can be in the form of a pond, a fountain, or a humble birdbath. Almost any type of container can be converted into an effective birdbath. An ideal container has a rough, gently sloping bottom to provide a variety of water depths for both big and small birds. The roughness on the bottom will help keep your guests from slipping. Concrete is a great material for a birdbath. It can be cast into a wide variety of shapes, is virtually impervious to the elements, and almost automatically has a rough surface.

The birdbath shown here is quite different from the precast units available at your local garden center. Rather than following the typical dish shape, its form has an architectural feel almost like a Greek fountain. The steps offer a variety of depths for different sizes of birds. It is meant to rest directly on the ground or to be sunken slightly below grade, forming a small oasis within your garden. When you place a birdbath or feeder on the ground, be sure to position it away from low shrubbery or other spots where predators may hide.

MAKING THE POUR

The trickiest part of making these birdbaths is getting them to come out of the form after the concrete has cured. Wax the form pieces well with paste wax before filling the form with concrete. The wax will prevent the concrete from sticking to the form pieces. 🐝

HAVE ON HAND:

- ▶ Tape measure
- ▶ Circular saw
- ▶ Block plane
- ▶ Hammer
- ▶ Screw gun/drill and bits
- ▶ 1-inch screws
- ▶ 16d staging nails
- ▶ Scraps of lumber and plywood
- ▶ Prebagged concrete (sand mix)
- ▶ Wheelbarrow
- ▶ Trowel

- ▶ Shovel

Cutting List:
- ▶ Form piece A: ½ x 12 x 21 inches
- ▶ Form piece B: ¾ x 7½ x 21 inches
- ▶ Form piece C: ¾ x 5½ x 21 inches
- ▶ Base: ¾ x 19 x 27 inches
- ▶ Two sides: 27-inch-long 2 x 4s
- ▶ Two ends: 16-inch-long 2 x 4s

Cut the form pieces to size. Bevel the long edges a few degrees off square so the pieces will come free from the concrete.

Stack form pieces together, centering them from wide to narrow with ends flush and wide side of each down. Fasten pieces with 1-inch screws.

Cut a slight relief bevel on the ends of the stack with your circular saw. Tilt the blade slightly off square; trim all three pieces at once.

Attach the stack of form boards to the base with screws. The stack should be centered from end to end and from side to side.

Nail the sides to the ends to form a rectangular frame. Use duplex staging nails so that you will be able to easily pull the nails later.

Nail the base to the frame with more duplex staging nails. Two nails per side are plenty.

Mix concrete according to directions on the bag. Pack concrete onto the form boards with a trowel, then finish filling the form with a shovel.

After concrete sets, pull duplex nails to remove frame from casting. Gently pry base and form boards away to free your new birdbath.

HERE'S HOW

PREVENTING LEAKS

Concrete is a porous material by its very nature, so some leakage is almost inevitable. As the concrete cures in the form, the birdbath may also develop some hairline cracks. If you have trouble with water slowly leaking from your birdbath, you may need to apply a sealer. Most hardware stores carry a variety of products that you can apply to concrete to make it more watertight. Follow the directions on the label.

Alternatives

A FREE-FORM BIRDBATH

It may be that you would like to make your own concrete birdbath, but you don't want to go through the time and effort of building a wooden form to make just one birdbath. With just a minimum of preparation, you can cast a free-form birdbath. Start by digging a shallow hole in the soil. Spread a piece of plastic over the hole—a trash bag will do. This will keep the water in the concrete from running off into the soil too quickly.

Mix up a bag of sand-mix concrete. Try to keep it on the dry side so that it will hold its shape when you pour it. Shovel the concrete into the depression you made in the ground. Use a small concrete trowel to spread it around, hollowing out an area in the center. If the concrete is too wet, you may find that it tends to settle back into this hollow. If this is the case, let the concrete sit for 15 or 20 minutes, then come back and trowel it again. As the concrete begins to set up, it will be much more likely to stay where you put it. You can create your own personal design for the birdbath by adding items such as seashells or pebbles to the surface of your casting. Just press the items into the wet concrete. ✺

CHOOSING PRECAST CONCRETE

Working with concrete—building the forms, mixing up the batch, and making the pour—can be a lot of fun, but it can be frustrating and messy, too. It takes experimentation to get results that are more or less predictable. When you first start out, you should expect that some of your projects won't turn out exactly as planned. In fact, some of the things you make may turn out to be just plain unattractive—and there is nothing like having your mistakes cast in stone! It is worth persevering, however, as after a few pours you'll soon be getting the results you want.

If you aren't interested in the process of pouring concrete, there is another option. Many companies specialize in making cast concrete lawn ornaments, with birdbaths being one of the perennial favorites. Most garden centers stock a few of these sculptural pieces. You may also run across an establishment that specializes in concrete artistry. You should be able to find a piece that suits your taste, whether you're looking for formal elegance or whimsical humor. Don't worry about offending your feathered guests. They'll be grateful for the water no matter what the basin looks like. ✺

Creating a Butterfly Haven

With its steeply pitched roof and trio of entry slots, this diminutive structure has all the charm and presence of a simple country church. For its beauty alone, it will make a fine addition to your landscape. But it also has a more practical side. Nestled in among the foliage of your garden, it will provide a safe haven for those delicate, beautifully marked creatures known as butterflies. In addition to the enjoyment they bring to a garden, butterflies serve as invaluable pollinators as they float from flower to flower.

The haven has two key features that make it attractive to butterflies. First, its wooden walls provide good insulation, helping to maintain a moderate inside temperature. And second, the haven can be filled with bark, which butterflies seem to enjoy.

If you decide to build a butterfly haven, you may also want to grow some plants and bushes that are naturally attractive to butterflies. This will increase your chances of creating a true butterfly sanctuary. There are some suggestions for plants on page 83; you can also check with your local garden center or nursery to see what kind of plants will do well in your area.

BUILDING THE HAVEN

Build the butterfly haven from a naturally weather-resistant wood such as cedar or redwood. These woods will gradually weather to a handsome silvery gray. Or, if you prefer, you can paint the haven to complement the color scheme of your garden. ✿

HAVE ON HAND:

- ▶ Tape measure
- ▶ Protractor
- ▶ T-bevel
- ▶ Table saw and saber saw
- ▶ Hammer
- ▶ Coping saw
- ▶ Screw gun/drill and bits
- ▶ Wood glue
- ▶ 8d galvanized finish nails
- ▶ 2-inch screws
- ▶ Wood preservative or paint

- ▶ 4-foot-long 1 x 8
- ▶ 4-foot-long 1 x 6

Cutting List:

- ▶ Long roof: 13¾-inch-long 1 x 8
- ▶ Short roof: 12⅜-inch-long 1 x 8
- ▶ Two front/back pieces: 14-inch-long 1 x 6s
- ▶ Two sides: ¾ x 4⅜ x 5 inches
- ▶ Bottom: ¾ x 4⅜ x 4 inches

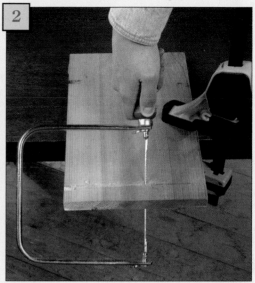

Cut the two roof pieces to size. Using a protractor and sliding T-bevel as a guide, mark a 56° angle cut on one end of each piece.

Glue and nail the two roof pieces together. Predrill the holes to avoid splitting the wood.

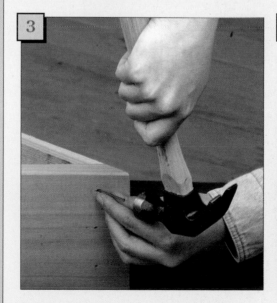

Clamp pieces to a workbench and use a coping saw to cut the bevels marked in Step 1.

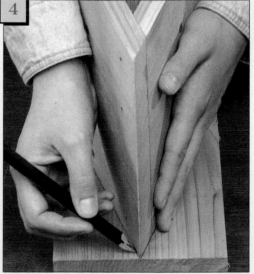

To cut front and back to size, center the roof on the pieces and trace the angle. Cut along the lines with a saber saw.

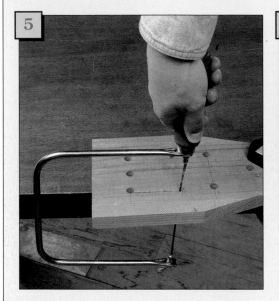

Drill ⅜-inch holes in front to mark the ends of the slots. Mark side slots 4 inches long; center slot, 6 inches long. Cut slots with a coping saw.

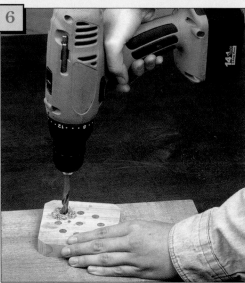

Cut sides and bottom to size. Cut corners off bottom; drill a series of ⅜-inch holes for drainage. Screw sides to bottom.

Screw front and back to sides and bottom, then screw roof to assembled house. Most of the overhang should be in the front.

Seal house with a nontoxic wood preservative or paint to match the color scheme of your house or garden. Attach the house to a post.

HERE'S HOW

MOUNTING THE HAVEN

You can attach your butterfly haven to a wooden post, as shown here, or you can mount it atop a length of galvanized steel water pipe. Purchase a 4- to 5-foot length and drive it into the ground, using a block of scrap wood to protect the threads. Screw a floor flange to the top of the pipe, then drive screws up through the flange into the bottom of the haven.

Alternatives

PLANTS TO ATTRACT BUTTERFLIES

One of the nice aspects of a butterfly haven is that the plants in it bear some of the most attractive, fragrant blossoms in the garden. Different butterflies will appear throughout the warmer months, so be sure to plant flowering plants that offer blossoms throughout the growing season.

Flowers for spring include lilacs, viburnums, magnolias, violets, lupines, peonies, dianthus, and an array of annuals you can purchase from local garden centers, such as impatiens, marigolds, and sweet alyssum.

As summer approaches, a wide range of perennials flower, including bee balm, Shasta daisies, lavender, passionflower, black-eyed Susan, milkweed, coreopsis, and heliotrope. Butterfly bush and vines such as jasmine accent summer annuals such as zinnias, petunias, and verbena.

From late summer to fall, butterflies enjoy the blooms of garden phlox, goldenrod, asters, boltonia, trumpet vine, honeysuckle, yarrow, and Joe-Pye weed. Pentas, lantana, and calamondin can be planted outside in warmer climates or grown in containers in colder regions.

A garden filled with beautiful flowers is a show-stopper all by itself. Add the shimmering wings of butterflies to the display, and the result is nothing short of magic.

BLACK-EYED SUSAN
Rudbeckia spp.
24–30 inches tall
Zones 4–9
Perennials and biennials with lance-shaped basal leaves and strong, often branched stems topped with solitary, daisylike blossoms with golden yellow, ray flowers surrounding a dark brown central disk; moist, average soil; full sun to very light shade.

LILAC
Syringa patula **'Miss Kim'**
5–8 feet tall
Zones 5–8
Spreading shrub with small, glossy green leaves and brownish purple twigs; in spring bears delicate panicles of four-petaled, richly scented pale lilac-pink flowers; rich, evenly moist, slightly acid to alkaline soil; full sun; mulch in spring and fall.

BUTTERFLY WEED
Asclepias tuberosa
20–30 inches tall
Zones 4–9
Erect perennial with deep green, lance-shaped leaves and thick stems with milky sap; distinctive, orange-red flowers appear from midsummer to fall; rich, evenly moist, well-drained soil; full sun.

COREOPSIS
Coreopsis grandiflora **'Early Sunrise'**
15–18 inches tall
Zones 4–9
Clump-forming perennial with lance-shaped deep green leaves and pliant stems topped with solitary, semidouble, golden yellow flowers from late spring to late summer; evenly moist, well-drained soil; full sun. Deadhead spent blooms to prolong flowering period.

HELIOTROPE
Heliotropium arborescens **'Fragrant Delight'**
18–40 inches tall
Zones 9–11
Shrubby, often short-lived plants with deep green to reddish green, textured leaves; dense clusters of richly scented white, lavender-blue, or violet flowers in summer; consistently moist, fertile soil during growing season, slightly drier conditions during winter; full sun.

Enjoying Your Yard and Garden

As relaxing as gardening is, it is also nice to take some time every day to simply enjoy the space you have created. Take a minute, or four, to sit down and listen to the wind in the leaves. Or, stroll along the paths, pausing to admire each scene as it comes into view.

You can build any number of things that will help you enjoy your garden. These include various pieces of outdoor furniture, decorative accents, and even landscaping features to draw attention to and better define certain areas. You might think of your garden as an additional room (or rooms) in your house, albeit a comparatively large room. As a room, you can furnish it with the same sort of things you would have indoors—seating, art objects, tables, and the like. Place these items throughout your garden as you would in a room inside.

As you think about what sorts of things to build for your garden, consider the overall garden plan. Consider where you might want to put a bench for a quiet moment of reflection, or where you might install a sundial to draw attention to a particularly stunning flower bed. You might even want to build some sort of gateway to serve as a friendly sentinel standing guard along the garden path. ❧

Making a Porch Swing

There are few more pleasant ways of whiling away a warm summer evening than sitting on a porch swing sipping lemonade as the sun goes down. Porch swings allow you time to sit back and reflect on life, read a book, or just doze for a while. And no one can rightfully accuse you of being lazy—you are swinging, after all.

A porch swing can be as elaborate or as simple as you prefer. The one here is on the simple side, but it is quite comfortable and can be built with a minimum of tools and materials. It was built from #2 pine and fir framing lumber and then painted with several coats of exterior enamel. You could also use a hardwood such as oak and give the swing a clear finish to allow the beauty of the wood to show through.

If you don't have a porch, don't think that you have to miss out on the fun of having a porch swing. You can just as easily hang the swing from a tree, or even from a swing set in place of the uncomfortable strap swings that purchased sets usually have.

MAKING THE SWING

It is critical that the rib assemblies match, even if they don't taper as specified. So make one pair carefully, then use that pair as a pattern for the rest. 🌿

HAVE ON HAND:

- ▶ Tape measure
- ▶ Speed square
- ▶ Circular saw
- ▶ Screw gun/drill and bits
- ▶ Saber saw
- ▶ Block plane
- ▶ Chisel
- ▶ 2-inch-long ⅜-inch bolts with washers and nuts
- ▶ 1⅝- and 3-inch screws
- ▶ Four 3-inch-long ½-inch eyebolts with eight nuts and washers
- ▶ 24 feet of chain
- ▶ Three open links

- ▶ Wood glue
- ▶ 12-foot-long 2 x 4
- ▶ 4-foot-long 1 x 3
- ▶ Three 8-foot-long 1 x 4s

Cutting List:
- ▶ Three back ribs: 19-inch-long 2 x 4s
- ▶ Three seat ribs: 21-inch-long 2 x 4s
- ▶ Spacer: 45½-inch-long 1 x 3
- ▶ Four seat boards: 4-foot-long 1 x 4s
- ▶ Two back boards: 4-foot-long 1 x 4s

Set circular saw to cut halfway through ribs. Make repeated square cuts to create rabbet for lap joint; remove pieces with chisel.

Taper seat ribs from full width at the shoulder of the rabbet to 3 inches at the end. The back ribs taper from full width to 1¾ inches.

Hold ribs together at the lap joint and drill holes through them for carriage bolts. Apply glue where surfaces will join, then bolt pieces together.

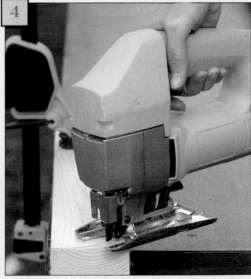

Cut 1¾ inches off the end of the center seat rib. Round off the corners of all the ribs with a saber saw.

Center the spacer on the center rib assembly.
Screw it to the center seat rib, flush with top.
Screw outer ribs to ends of the spacer.

Center the seat boards on the ribs and screw
them in place. Round over the front edge of the
seat with a block plane.

Drill through outer seat and back ribs for eyebolts. Center the holes about 1½ inches in from
the ends. Install the eyebolts.

Attach 48-inch chains to front eyebolts and
41-inch chains to back ones. Join these chains
to those hanging from the ceiling.

HERE'S HOW

MAKING IT COMFORTABLE

**Two factors will determine how
comfortable your swing will be:**
the angle between the seat and the
back, and the angle at which the swing
hangs. The seat-to-back angle can be
adjusted by changing how much the
pieces taper. As designed here, this
angle seems about right, but you can
adjust the shape of the pieces if you
desire. The angle at which the swing
hangs is determined by the length of
the chains running to the eyebolts.
Adjust the chain lengths a link or two
at a time until the swing hangs at an
angle that you find comfortable.

Alternatives

TREE SWINGS

As you're wandering about your property, keep an eye looking up in the trees. What you're searching for is a stout branch (5 inches or more in diameter) about 8 to 10 feet high, coming more or less straight out from the tree parallel to the ground, with few or no branches directly beneath it. If you are fortunate enough to have a tree with such a branch, you are almost obligated to hang a swing from it. And if that branch happens to overlook a picturesque spot such as a stream or a pond, then a swing is a necessity.

Keep in mind that what we're talking about here is a relaxing kind of swing—a place where you can sit back and contemplate on a warm afternoon. If what you have in mind is a little more adventurous, you should set your sights a little higher up in the trees. Kids won't be satisfied with a low, gentle tree swing. For a real crowd pleaser, you will need to find a swing branch that is a good 20 feet up (and 30 or 40 feet is even better). If you have such a branch, you're looking at the possibility of creating a real world-class tree swing. All you have to do is trim back the vegetation from around the base of the tree, hang the swing, and let 'em fly. ❦

A SLING SWING

If your tastes lean to the informal, you might consider building this swing. It is a hybrid swing/hammock that combines some of the best features of each. Because it is made of individual slats that are supported by ropes, the swing tends to conform to the shape of your body as you sit on it in the way that a hammock does. But because the slats are rigid, they offer more support than a hammock's ropes do. The swing is also much less likely to tip you out of it than your average hammock.

The wooden slats that make up the seat of this swing have holes drilled at each end. The corners of the slats are rounded over with a router to make them a bit more comfortable. The slats are threaded on two lengths of rope, which are attached to spreader bars above. The swing is hung from lines running from the spreaders to the ceiling of a porch or the branch of a tree. If you want to experiment, you could increase the number of slats in the seat and create a wooden hammock. Be careful how you hang such a swing, however. If you hang it like a regular hammock, it could provide quite a knock on the head to someone who is unfortunate enough to spill out of it. ❦

Building a Garden Bench

Benches in a garden draw people in and create the sense that your garden is a space to be lived in as an extension of your house. The bench pictured is designed to be placed in the corner of a patio or deck or tucked into the turn of a pathway. It can be a quiet spot to catch one's breath, a focal point to sit and take in all that is happening, or simply a place to sit down and take off muddy garden boots. Whatever its purpose, it is a bench that is both easy to make and handsome to own.

While the striking geometric pattern of the seat may look complicated, it is really made up of a number of identical pieces assembled in a repetitive manner. With a little glue and a few screws to hold the pieces together, you can assemble the entire bench over the course of a weekend and still have time for a Sunday afternoon picnic. You can build the bench with a few basic hand and power tools, but it does help to have access to a table saw for making the numerous angled cuts and sawing the many duplicate parts. ❧

MAKING THE BENCH

The bench pictured is made from cedar, which holds up well but can be expensive. One option is to buy a lesser grade and cut around the defects. ✿

HAVE ON HAND:

- Tape measure
- Table saw
- Screw gun/drill and bits
- Square
- Sliding bevel
- Weatherproof glue
- 2- and 3-inch screws
- Three 8-foot-long 2x4s
- 6-foot-long 1x6
- 8-foot-long 2x6
- 6-foot-long 1x3

Cutting List:
- Three long slats: 1½ x 1½ x 48 inches
- Three slats 1½ x 1½ x 34½ inches and three slats 1½ x 1½ x 21 inches
- Twenty-two spacers: ¾ x 1½ x 5¼ inches
- Long spacer: ¾ x 1½ x 6 inches
- Point: ¾ x 1½ x 1½ inches
- Four runners: 1½ x 2½ x 26½ inches
- Four legs: 1½ x 5 x 11 inches
- Stretcher: 37½-inch-long 1x3
- Back stretcher: 11-inch-long 1x3

Cut slats and spacers to size. Cut ends of all spacers at 45° on the table saw or chop saw. (On the long spacer, the angles are opposing.)

Cut ends of first long slat at 45°. Glue and screw four spacers to the slat, two 1½ inches in from ends, the others 12¾ inches in.

Place second long slat against spacers. Use a sliding bevel to mark end cuts and spacer locations, following established pattern. Cut.

Screw second slat in place. Add next set of spacers. Continue building seat this way. (Center spacers end with long spacer and then the point.)

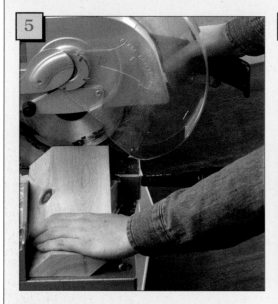

Bevel the edges of the legs with the blade on your table saw tilted to 45°, then cut the legs to length.

To make base, crosscut the ends of the runners at 45° to match the legs. Screw the runners to the legs.

Screw the base to the underside of the top. The outside edges of the top runners should align with the outer ends of the outside spacers.

Cut stretchers to size, beveling their ends at 45°. Glue and screw them to legs midway between top and bottom runners, front and back.

HERE'S HOW

FINISHING THE BENCH

When you work with weather-resistant woods such as cedar and redwood, it really isn't necessary to put a finish on them to protect them from the elements. Left alone, these species will gradually turn a lovely silver gray. But if you prefer the "natural" look of freshly milled wood, there are a number of products you can apply to help prevent weathering. Ask at your local hardware store about clear finishes for protecting cedar and/or redwood siding. These are usually easy to apply and can be touched up with a minimal amount of preparation.

Alternatives

A BENCH WITH STONE "LEGS"

One of the biggest problems with wooden outdoor furnishings is rot. This is especially true for wood that is left in contact with the ground, such as the legs of benches and other furniture. Even woods that are naturally resistant to rot tend to decay quickly if they are placed in contact with soil. One option is to use pressure-treated wood, but you need to be extremely careful when working with it and should try to avoid letting dust from it come in contact with your skin.

Instead, you might try combining wood with other materials in your projects. Use decay-resistant materials such as concrete for parts that are susceptible to rot, and wood for the parts that aren't as vulnerable to moisture. The bench shown here makes use of two stacks of wide and flat stones for its "legs" and slats of redwood for the bench top itself.

The stones are heavy enough to stay upright by themselves, so you won't need to attach the top slats to them. This makes the bench relatively easy to move for mowing purposes. It also allows you to store the top for the winter in a very small amount of space. ❧

A TWIG BENCH

If you find the amount of woodworking involved in building a bench from lumber a bit intimidating, consider building one from sticks and twigs. Building furniture from twigs and other bits of trees is a craft that dates back many years. It requires few tools—a pruning saw, a hammer, perhaps an ax and a pair of loppers—and even fewer materials—twigs, vines, and an assortment of nails. The process is quite creative and intuitive; you cut the pieces to fit and attach them to one another as you go. You can start with a bench that you find comfortable and use it as a model, or simply build one to fit to your body. Either way, you'll end up with a unique piece of garden furniture.

The hardest part of building with twigs can be finding just the right material to begin with. You might try checking with local farmers. They often have willow trees growing along waterways and would be quite happy to let you cut them. You might also talk to local landscaping contractors, who might allow you to pick through their trimmings before they make it to the chipper. Many municipalities have sites for dropping off garden waste that can provide a steady stream of fresh material free for the taking. ❧

Laying a Faux Stone Wall

With low stone walls, you can create some stunning landscaping effects. But when you go to check the prices of stones at your local building center, you may end up a little stunned yourself. Even one small wall's worth of man-made stones can be prohibitively expensive. But for about one-quarter the price—plus a little time and energy—you can cast your own concrete landscaping blocks that will work every bit as well as those available commercially.

The first step is to build one or two reusable forms in which to cast the blocks. You can make blocks in any shape, but trapezoid-shaped blocks seem to work best for building gently curving walls. Note that the forms are not actually fastened together but are held in place with clamps. This way, you can easily take the forms apart to release the blocks. You'll also find that wetting the form pieces before filling them with concrete will make it much easier to remove them after the concrete sets.

Plan the basic path of your wall before you start casting the stones. As you build up a small stock of stones, you can begin to set them in place, shaping the wall as you go. ✺

MAKING THE STONES

Once you have made a form (or two) you can go into the stone-making business. One 60-pound bag of concrete will make about four stones. You can also make custom-sized stones to add variety. Simply move the dividers closer together for smaller stones or farther apart for bigger ones. You can also vary the depth of the concrete to make thinner stones. ❦

HAVE ON HAND:

- Tape measure
- Circular saw
- Heavy-duty black plastic
- Carver's gouge or butt chisel
- Hammer
- Clamps
- Concrete mix
- Concrete trowel
- Spade
- Gravel and sand
- Level

- ¾-inch plywood, 2 x 4 feet
- 10-foot-long 2 x 4

Cutting List:
- Base: ¾ x 10 x 30 inches
- Two sides: 30-inch-long 2 x 4s
- Three dividers: 7½-inch-long 2 x 4s
- Eight corner blocks

Cut the base and sides to size. Wrap the base in a layer of heavy-duty black plastic to protect it from the water in the concrete.

Bevel ends of dividers at about 80°. Hold form together and mark where dividers go. Wide part of opening is about 11 inches.

Disassemble the form and carve some texture into the side pieces with either a carver's gouge or a regular butt chisel.

Clamp the form together and place it on the base (no need to attach it). Tap the pieces with a hammer to make sure they are sitting flat.

Cut corner blocks. Mix half a bag of concrete; trowel some concrete into each corner to hold corner blocks in place.

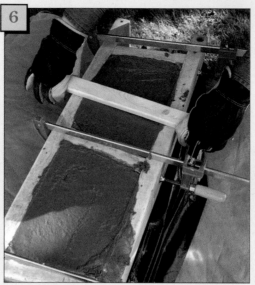

Finish filling the form, then level the top of the concrete with a piece of scrap wood. Let the concrete set overnight.

Use garden hose or rope to mark where your wall will go. Strip the sod along marked area and make a trench about 6 inches deep.

Fill trench with 4 inches of gravel, for drainage. Top with 2 inches of sand to make leveling the stones easier.

For straight sections, lay blocks so wide and narrow sides alternate. For convex curves, place stones wide side out; for concave curves, vice versa.

Lay stones so each course laps joints of those below. Align edges and check to be sure the wall is level and plumb.

Alternatives

WOODEN RETAINING WALLS

Sloping sites present both a challenge and a design opportunity. One way to deal with a slope is to dig in some terraces, with a series of retaining walls to keep erosion at bay. Retaining walls can be built from concrete, stone, old tires, or, as shown, landscape timbers. The resulting flat areas make ideal places to garden, and the various levels give you a chance to make your garden much more three-dimensional.

When building a wooden retaining wall, choose timbers that have been pressure treated and that are rated for ground contact. Cut in the terraces and dig away the soil from behind the area where the wall will eventually go. Also dig a trench along where the timbers are to be placed. Fill the trench with gravel (for drainage) and begin setting the timbers in place. As you add timbers, check with a level to make sure the wall remains level and plumb.

Spike the timbers together with long nails. Every few feet, place a timber perpendicular to the main wall extending into the slope. When you backfill (put back the excavated material), these perpendicular timbers will help keep the wall upright. Backfill behind the wall with gravel almost to the top, then finish off with topsoil. ❧

WORKING WITH NATURAL STONE

Cast concrete blocks and landscaping timbers make excellent retaining walls and raised beds, but for a sense of rustic charm and timelessness, it is hard to beat the look of a dry-laid stone wall. Stone blends in easily with the natural landscape, and it will look like it has been there for many years almost immediately. As an added gardening benefit, stone walls have numerous nooks and crannies that are perfect spots for growing a variety of creeping plants. In time, lichens and mosses may decide on their own to join your vertical rock garden.

Before starting any stonework, keep in mind that the individual stones can be quite heavy. You'll need a healthy back and strong legs to get the job done. If you have doubts about your ability to move any stones, get a helper to give you a hand with the big ones. Wearing gloves is strongly recommended as you begin laying up the stones. You should also be aware that the materials for even a modest project can weigh several tons. If you have to purchase stone, you may want to work on a small scale at first to learn just how far a ton of stone will go before you commit yourself to a large and potentially expensive project. ❧

Constructing a Sundial

In a garden, the concept of time is not nearly so rigid as it is in the workaday world. What better place, then, for a timekeeping device as archaic as the sundial? Unlike a digital watch slicing time into fractions of a second, a sundial speaks through shadow of the subtle yet relentless movement of the sun across the sky. While your wrist watch may provide a more precise reading, the shadow on a sundial may be a more genuine indication of how the hours pass into days and the days into seasons.

Sundials have a long tradition in landscape design. Deciding where to place yours can be part of the fun. Does it belong in the center of a bed of flowers, or at the intersection of two pathways? Regardless of where you set it, your sundial is sure to become one of the focal points of your garden.

The sundial pictured here began with a metal sundial purchased from a local garden center. The base was then cast and assembled with strong, basic materials—concrete, copper, and steel. The result is a monument that will stand up to the elements and keep watch over your garden for many seasons. ❧

CASTING THE STAND

Choose two plastic flowerpots as molds, and treat the insides of the pots with paste wax. 🌺

HAVE ON HAND:

- Tape measure
- Compass
- Protractor
- Hacksaw
- Drill with bits
- File
- Small trowel
- Seven ¾-inch PVC pipe caps
- Plastic flowerpots
- ½-inch electrical conduit, 36-inch piece
- Duct tape
- Four 4-inch-long ⅜-inch bolts with nuts
- Three 8-inch-long ⅜-inch bolts with nuts

- ⅜-inch threaded rod, three 36-inch pieces
- Two bags of sand-mix concrete
- 2-inch copper pipe, three 24-inch pieces
- Sundial

Cutting List:

- Top disk: ¾ x 5½-inch dia.
- Bottom disk: ¾ x 6½-inch dia.
- ½-inch dia. pipe spacers: four top spacers, 2 inches long; three bottom spacers, 6½ inches long

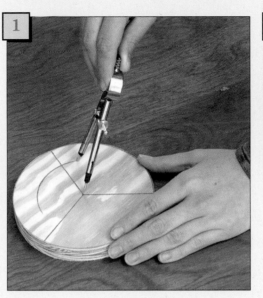

Divide each disk into thirds with protractor. Draw second circle on disks: 3⅝-inch diameter on top, 5½-inch on bottom to mark drill points.

With top and bottom disks centered on over-turned tray and bowl, drill three ⅜-inch holes at marked points. Center a fourth hole in top disk.

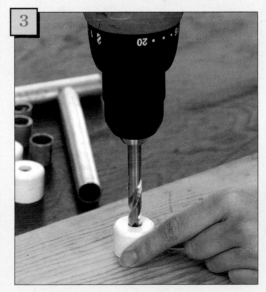

Drill a ⅜-inch hole through center of each pipe cap. Cut electrical conduit to length to make pipe spacers. File rough edges smooth.

Slip a cap over each bolt, followed by a spacer. Push bolts through the pot and disk and fasten them with nuts. Seal the caps with duct tape.

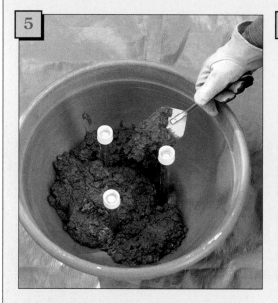

Mix the concrete according to the instructions. Fill the forms a little at a time, trying not to leave any voids around the spacers.

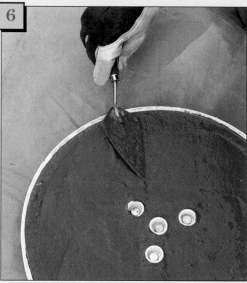

When the concrete begins to set, smooth around the perimeter of the top casting, easing the edge where it meets the pot.

After the concrete sets, unbolt the casting from the forms. Slide threaded rods up through the base. Add the copper pipes, then the top.

Slide a bolt up through the hole in the center of the top casting and bolt the sundial in place.

HERE'S HOW

PLACING YOUR SUNDIAL

For the most accurate readings, you should make sure your sundial is level with the gnomon (or pointer) pointing at true north, not magnetic north. To find true north, wait until noon, then turn the gnomon until its shadow falls upon itself. Due to variations in the solar day, there are only four days a year when the readings on your sundial will match those on your watch. They are April 15, June 15, September 1, and December 24. Remember to make adjustments for Daylight Savings Time.

Alternatives

DECORATIVE GARDEN ADDITIONS

Sundials and birdbaths aren't the only decorative items you can place in your garden. Look through a few garden supply catalogs and you'll find hundreds of suitable objects, ranging from classic statuary and sculpture to large ceramic vases and urns to gazing balls and whimsical garden critters. As you decide which accents you'd like, think about how you want the object to be seen. Will it be a focal point in your garden? If so, you'll want a fairly large item so it won't be overwhelmed by nearby plantings. Smaller items will work better for complementing nearby plants and trees.

Also consider your audience. Are you adding items to your garden simply to augment the natural beauty of what you have grown, or are they supposed to lend an air of formality? Perhaps you would like accents that will surprise and amuse those who view them. Imagine the delight of a visiting child who happens upon a statue of a garden gnome under the wide-spreading leaves of a fern or who spies a goofy gargoyle standing watch over a path. No matter what your intent, take your time and enjoy the search for the perfect items to add to your garden. ❧

A CLASSIC SUNDIAL

Along with the more familiar sundials available, you may come across a type of sundial known as an armillary sphere. Developed centuries ago by early French astronomers, these unusual looking instruments were used at night to help chart the movement of planets, stars, and other celestial bodies. When viewed during the day, an armillary makes a perfectly good sundial. (Don't forget that the sun qualifies as a celestial object.) To position the armillary so it functions properly, you should turn it until the center arrow points toward the North Star.

Not only will the armillary sundial aid you in observing various heavenly bodies, but it will also lend a formal elegance to its surroundings. You can place this sundial almost anywhere in your garden for an unusual, eye-catching feature. To be the most functional, it should be in a place that gets at least some sunlight during the day. If you are interested in "reading" the data from the shadows on the dial, you should also position it where you easily can get close to it. Armillary spheres often come with simple pole or tripod bases, or you can consider casting a base for your sundial from concrete. ❧

Fashioning a Gateway Arbor

An arbor, or archway, makes a great entry to a garden, helping to define the space and beckoning to passersby to come and explore. Plant some vines at the base, and in a few years you'll have a living piece of architecture standing sentinel over your garden sanctuary. Or place the arbor deep within the garden along one of its pathways to add a highlight to the journey. Wherever you decide it should go, choose a style that fits in with the landscape. This rustic arbor will fit right into a wild and woolly woodland garden.

The twig construction featured here is a fun, fast, and simple way to work. You'll need little more than a pruning saw, a hammer, and some nails to get started. If you have a wooded area on your property, you may already have a sufficient supply of material. If not, ask a local landowner. Explain what you're doing, and chances are you'll be able to cut all the material you need. The saplings you'll find growing at the edge of woods should yield a nice variety of lengths and diameters of sticks to choose from. Cut a few extra to replace the inevitable mistakes.

BUILDING THE ARBOR

Don't get hung up on the exact dimensions here. Cut your materials, then work with what you have. You may find an elegantly bent limb for an arch or a crotch for a natural brace. 🌾

HAVE ON HAND:

- ▶ Tape measure
- ▶ Pruning saw
- ▶ Hammer
- ▶ Screw gun/drill and bits
- ▶ Hatchet
- ▶ 8d and 16d nails
- ▶ 1⅝- and 3-inch screws
- ▶ ¼-inch rebar, four 12-inch pieces

Cutting List:

- ▶ Four legs: 2½-inch dia. x 88 inches
- ▶ Four crosspieces: 1½-inch dia. x 25½ inches

- ▶ Two diagonals: 1½-inch dia. x 67 inches
- ▶ Two top crosspieces: 1½-inch dia. x 30 inches
- ▶ Two lower arches: 2-inch dia. x 48 inches
- ▶ Two upper arches: 2-inch dia. x 63 inches
- ▶ Four braces: 1-inch dia. x 15 inches
- ▶ Twenty top pieces: 1½-inch dia. x 30 inches

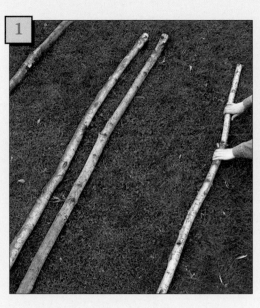

Assemble the two side "ladders" at the same time so they will be nearly symmetrical. Start with the leg pairs lying side by side.

Nail the four crosspieces to legs, about 8 inches from the top and bottom. Predrill the holes to prevent splitting.

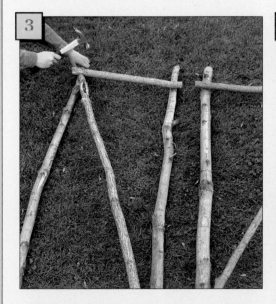

Hold diagonals in place and cut them to fit in between the crosspieces. Make sure ladders are basically square, then nail diagonals in place.

Add the top crosspieces. They should be centered from end to end on the legs about 3 inches down from the top.

Prop ladders on their sides, about 36 inches apart. Attach upper and lower arches with screws to avoid banging the assembled ladders.

Cut the ends of the braces to 45°. Nail or screw them in the corners between the lower arches and the legs.

Spread out the top pieces on top of the upper arch, spacing them evenly. Nail or screw them in place.

Drill a ¼-inch hole at an angle through each leg and drive a rebar spike into it. Set arbor in place and force spikes into ground.

HERE'S HOW
FASTENING STICKS

It is amazing what you can build by simply nailing or screwing twigs and sticks together without any other real joinery. Put together a supply of fasteners of various lengths to work with. For nails, 4d, 8d, 12d, and 16d will give you a good selection. For screws, stock 1⅝, 2, and 3 inches. For outdoor use, galvanized fasteners will last longer than nongalvanized ones.

When you are working, predrill the holes to keep the wood from splitting. If possible, drive two fasteners into each joint at slightly opposing angles for the strongest connection.

Alternatives

PLANTS FOR A GATEWAY ARBOR

The rustic style of a gateway arbor constructed from twigs is the perfect foil for a number of vining plants. Some vines will quickly cover the framework with layers of green foliage that give the arbor a shady, secretive ambiance. Suitable fast-growing vines include grape, five-leaf akebia (also called chocolate vine), Dutchman's pipe, Carolina jasmine, cross vine, Japanese and Chinese wisteria, and trumpet vine. These plants can weigh down an arbor or archway, so be liberal with the pruning shears and thin the plants periodically.

Some vines, such as climbing hydrangea and winter-creeper, grow much more slowly, and even though they can in time also become heavy, they require much less pruning than more vigorous vines. Some vines, such as climbing hydrangea, also have decorative bark that stands out against the backdrop of rustic garden accents.

Honeysuckle, passionflower, and clematis vines have slender stems that offer a graceful alternative to heavier vining plants. If you like to see the arch exposed during the winter months, grow annual vines for seasonal color such as scarlet runner bean, hyacinth bean, moonflower, morning glory, calabash gourd, and black-eyed Susan vine. ❧

FIVELEAF AKEBIA
Akebia quinata
10–20 feet tall
Zones 5–9
Climbing vine with hand-shaped leaves composed of five stout, round leaflets; russet-brown flowers have spicy fragrance; purplish fruit sometimes are borne in late summer to fall; evenly moist, well-drained, fertile soil; full sun to partial shade.

DUTCHMAN'S PIPE
Aristolochia macrophylla
20–25 feet tall
Zones 5–8
Vigorous, very fast-growing, twining vine with large, heart-shaped leaves that hide the small, greenish purple summer flowers; consistently moist, well-drained, rich soil; full sun to partial shade; best on strong support like sturdy arbor or pergola.

CLEMATIS
Clematis x jackmanii
8–10 feet tall
Zones 4–9
Slender deciduous vine with abundant, medium green leaves and large, very showy flowers from spring to fall; well-drained, rich soil; full sun to light shade; mulch to keep soil cool in summer and prevent heaving of soil in winter.

WINTERCREEPER
Euonymus fortunei
10–15 feet tall
Zones 5–9
Woody, evergreen ground cover or low shrub suitable for training on walls or other very sturdy supports; leaves are dark green, with some varieties having white or yellow variegated foliage; moist to dry, well-drained soil; full sun to partial shade.

CLIMBING HYDRANGEA
Hydrangea petiolaris
30–40 feet tall
Zones 4–9
Vigorous, deciduous woody vine with very attractive, cinnamon-colored bark and round to heart-shaped leaves; large, flat clusters of white flowers in summer; moist, well-drained soil in full sun to partial shade; best in sheltered location away from wind.

Hanging a Basket

The inspiration for this project came from the beautiful hanging baskets that grace the city of Vancouver. On a smaller scale, such baskets could add a bright touch at the end of your driveway or along your front walk. Garden centers often sell hanging baskets with plants in a variety of species and colors already growing inside. But before you can hang a basket, you need something to hang it from. This hanger is designed to accommodate up to four hanging baskets, although you don't have to use all four spaces for plants. Two hanging baskets accompanied by a hanging birdbath and a feeder would make a lovely addition to any garden.

At the heart of this hanger is a 9-foot, pressure-treated post. Try to find pressure-treated stock that is rated for ground contact, as the end of the post will be buried. The strips that run along each side of the post are also pressure-treated. They, as well as the small roof, serve primarily to dress up the post and make it look less utilitarian. The cross-bars are made from lengths of galvanized steel water pipe that should be stout enough to handle the weight of a good-sized hanging basket. ❦

MAKING THE HANGER

Pressure-treated lumber often isn't dry when you purchase it. As it dries, it tends to warp and twist, which will be quite noticeable with an upright post. Be selective when you buy your lumber and try to find the straightest pieces with the fewest checks (splits) you can. 🌺

HAVE ON HAND:

- Tape measure
- Speed square
- Circular saw
- Handsaw
- Hammer
- Electric drill with bits
- ¾-inch spade bit
- Center punch
- 8d galvanized finish nails
- ½-inch steel pipe, two 36-inch pieces
- Four eyebolts with nuts

- 10-foot-long pressure-treated 4 x 4
- Four 8-foot-long pressure-treated 1 x 2s
- 2-foot-long 1 x 8

Cutting List:
- Post: 9-foot-long 4 x 4
- Four strips: 8-foot-long 1 x 2s
- Two roof pieces: 6-inch-long 1 x 8s

Cut the post to length. Then tilt the blade on your circular saw to 45° and cut two faces at one end to form a peak.

Nail the strips to the sides of the post, centering them from side to side. Run the ends of strips slightly beyond the peaked end of the post.

Cut the ends of the strips off with a handsaw to match the angle of the peak.

Drill holes for the pipes, one 11 inches down from the peak, the other 17 inches down. Drill in from both sides to avoid splintering wood.

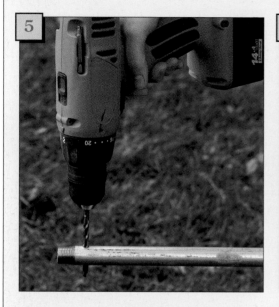

Use a center punch to dimple the pipes near their ends. Drill through the pipes at each dimple for the eyebolts.

Drive pipes through post, centering them from end to end. Slip eyebolts through their holes; tighten the nuts to lock them in place.

Cut the halves of the roof to size. Miter one end with your circular saw blade tilted to 45°. Nail pieces to top of post, with mitered edges together.

Dig a hole for the post about 2 feet deep. Hold the post upright as you fill in around it, tamping the soil down firmly as you go.

HERE'S HOW

ENTICING HUMMINGBIRDS

One potential ornament you might want to hang from your new hanger pole is a hummingbird feeder. Once you attract them, these diminutive birds will prove to be delightful company as they hover and flit about. Hummers are attracted to the colors red and orange, which is why feeders for them are often festooned with these bright hues. You can add to this attraction by growing red and orange flowers in your hanging baskets.

Alternatives

PLANTS FOR HANGING BASKETS

Few garden accents are as versatile as hanging baskets. A walk through a garden center nearly any time of year will find the greenhouse purlins crowded with colorful hanging baskets. Such a wealth of variety exists that just about anyone can find the right plant and hanging basket to complement any décor and design.

The best plants for hanging baskets have a vining or pendant habit with plenty of pliant stems to drape over the lip of the pot. Traditional favorites for shady decks and patios include impatiens, with abundant flowers from spring to frost, and fuchsia, a shrubby tender perennial with tubular flowers in a rainbow of vibrant shades. Partly sunny to sunny spots can be dressed up with ivy geranium, petunia, Swan River daisy, and scaevola.

Some hanging baskets, such as English ivy, glory bower, and Boston fern, can accentuate a shady outdoor location in warmer months and move indoors during colder times.

Hanging baskets often require only minimal care. Every week or so remove faded blossoms and fertilize once a month with a balanced water-soluble fertilizer. Keep soil evenly moist during the growing season, especially for plants in full sun. ❧

ENGLISH IVY
Hedera helix
3–10 feet tall
Zones 6–10
Very popular, woody evergreen vine with variable dark green or variegated leaves often with tapered lobes; rich, well-drained, moist soil; green varieties thrive in full sun to partial shade, variegated forms prefer bright, indirect light.

IVY GERANIUM
Pelargonium spp.
12–36 inches tall
Zones 10–11
Group of hybrids with trailing stems; ivy-shaped, deep green, often glossy leaves; and clusters of single or double flowers in white, pink, red, or violet. Well-drained, fertile soil; bright, indirect light; consistently moist soil during growing season, moderately dry during remainder of year.

IMPATIENS
Impatiens walleriana
10–24 inches tall
Zones 10–11
Weak-stemmed, tender perennial with dark green to reddish green leaves and flat, spurred flowers in colors from white, pink, red, lavender, and violet; rich, evenly moist soil; partial to full shade; protect from wind and drought.

GLORY BOWER
Clerodendrum thomsoniae
4–12 feet tall
Zones 10–11
Tropical, evergreen, climbing vine with green to reddish green leaves and distinctive blossoms with white bases beneath wheel of scarlet petals; rich, well-drained, evenly moist soil; full sun; prune to control size; repot and root prune yearly to avoid rootbound plants.

FUCHSIA
Fuchsia spp.
2–4 feet tall
Zones 9–11
Wide variety of free-flowering, woody shrubs with thin, pliant stems and dark green to reddish green leaves; long, tubular, single or double flowers in white, pink, red, violet, lavender, bicolors, and fuchsia; evenly moist, rich soil; partial to full shade; blossoms attract hummingbirds.

A Garden Table

Dining alfresco is one of the great joys of summer. Whether you set up on your deck or out in the garden, enjoying good food, drink, and company outside is an experience not to be missed. Unless you really would prefer to eat from a blanket spread on the ground every time, you're going to want some sort of an outdoor table. Fortunately, this is a piece of furniture that you can easily make in a day or two.

The table pictured is roomy enough for a party of four, although it could seat six in a pinch. You can also set it up with only a pair of place settings for a romantic dinner for two, of course. The table's base is made from standard framing lumber—2 x 3s and 2 x 4s. Try to choose the straightest, most knot-free pieces you can find. The top is a little more unusual. It is made from 5/4 pine—wood that is a full 1 inch thick. That extra quarter of an inch may not seem like much, but it makes the top seem so much more substantial than it would if made from ¾-inch material, yet not as clunky as it would be with 2 x 3 or 2 x 4 stock.

BUILDING THE TABLE

Be careful in cutting the ends of the feet and stretchers. Make two pairs of each, one with center notches facing up and the other with notches down. ❧

HAVE ON HAND:

- Tape measure
- Square
- T-bevel and protractor
- Circular saw
- Handsaw
- Chisel
- Screw gun/drill
- Pencil, string
- 1⅝- and 2½-inch screws
- Plastic glides
- Two 12-foot-long 2 x 4s
- Two 8-foot-long 2 x 3s
- Five 8-foot-long ⁵⁄₄ x 6s
- 8-foot-long 1 x 3

Cutting List:

- Four feet: 34-inch-long 2 x 4s
- Four stretchers: 46-inch-long 2 x 3s
- Four legs: 29¾-inch-long 2 x 4s
- Five long slats: 1 x 5½ x 49 inches
- Four short slats: 1 x 5½ x 40 inches
- Four short battens: 13-inch-long 1 x 3s
- Two long battens: 29¼-inch-long 1 x 3s

Score layout lines with a utility knife, and cut two notches at the center of each foot and stretcher. Clean up bottom of cut with a chisel.

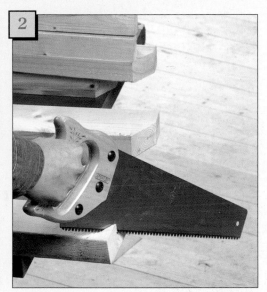

Cut a 30° taper on the ends of the feet and stretchers, leaving a flat end 1½ inches wide on the feet and 1 inch wide on the stretchers.

Assemble the feet and stretchers. Be careful with the piece of wood between the notches, as it is fragile. Reinforce joints with screws.

Cut ends of the legs off at 77°. Screw them in position 6 inches from ends of stretchers and 6⁷⁄₁₆ inches from ends of feet.

Lay out the top slats with 1/8-inch spacers. Using a pencil and 24 inches of string, draw a 48-inch circle on top. Cut and sand pieces to shape.

Reassemble the top upside down and center the base on it. Cut the battens to size and screw them to the slats to hold the slats in place.

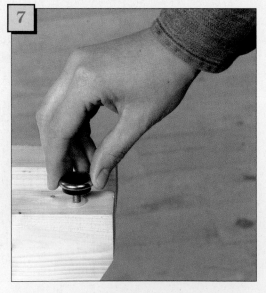

While the table is upside down, screw glides to the bottom of the feet. These will help the table sit flatter.

Drive screws down through the stretchers into the slats to anchor the top in place.

HERE'S HOW

ADDING AN UMBRELLA

This table design just happens to work perfectly for accommodating an umbrella. The square opening created where the feet and the stretchers intersect will hold the stem of an umbrella in place. The only thing you have to do is cut a round hole in the top—a task you can easily do with a hole saw in an electric drill. If you know you would like to install an umbrella, buy the umbrella before building the table, then adjust the space between the notches in the stretchers and feet to fit its stem perfectly.

Alternatives

DINING ALFRESCO

A deck isn't the only place that you might want to furnish with an outdoor table and chairs. The brilliant autumn foliage in this garden clearing makes a stunning backdrop for a small table with its matching benches. The ensemble turns this spot into an intimate picnic grove, perfect for a late October lunch. Placing a table out in your garden, rather than on a patio or porch, extends your living space even farther into the great outdoors. Imagine the peaceful feeling that you'll get when sitting down to a cup of hot cider on a crisp fall day as the leaves drop quietly from the trees, or from taking a few minutes in early spring to breathe in the scent of the garden as it awakens from its winter slumber.

The table shown here provides seating for four. It is approximately 3 feet square and is constructed of naturally weather-resistant cedar. The legs are 4 x 4s, the aprons are 2 x 4s, and the top is pieced together from 5/4 decking boards. The benches are made from 2 x 4s and 2 x 6s. The joints are screwed together with stainless steel fasteners. (Galvanized fasteners will leave dark streaks on cedar and other woods.) ❧

TWIG FURNITURE

The style of furniture that you should choose for your outdoor living spaces depends largely on your garden's design. In a formal garden, you'll need pieces with a more refined look. Traditional English garden benches come to mind, as do chairs made of ornate cast iron. In contrast, the wilder look of a country garden lends itself to less sophisticated furnishings. While the lines and design of a twig chair can be as graceful as those of a fine antique, the simple materials used give the piece a rustic air.

One of the fun things about twig furniture is how easy it is to build yourself. To make a chair, the easiest method is to base the dimensions on an existing chair that you find comfortable. Cut a supply of twigs and sticks, then start piecing together the basic framework. When deciding on the size of pieces to use, keep in mind a basic hierarchy—major structural elements should be thicker than lesser ones. To strengthen the structure, add diagonal braces. For curved pieces such as the rim of the small table in the photo, use fresh-cut stock and bend it to shape, fastening it to the rest of the structure to hold the desired form. ❧

Projects for the Hardworking Garden

If you do much gardening at all, chances are you have a few favorite tools that make your work that much easier and more enjoyable—a small spade that fits well in your hands, for example, or a pair of loppers that cuts cleanly. You already know how much tools like these can enhance your day. Well, there is no reason you cannot create some outdoor projects that will add to your gardening enjoyment in a similar manner.

Whether you build a bench to make repotting and starting plants that much easier, or a corral to keep your trash cans from blowing away, a few hours invested in shop time can produce a project that will provide years of service and make life that much simpler. As you page through the projects presented here, start thinking about what problems you have in your garden and how the right project might solve them.

Consider the jobs you put off because they are a nuisance—like turning the compost pile. Perhaps having a compost bin that you can move from one place to another would make that task a bit less tedious. You could fill the bin in place, then, when it is time to turn the pile, you could lift the bin and place it right next to the pile. Then simply shovel the pile into the bin for a complete turnover. A well-designed garden feature can often help your garden to produce more—and you to work less.

Concealing Trash Cans

Trash and recycling cans are a necessary part of modern life, but they aren't very attractive. Rather than put up with such an eyesore, why not build an attractive corral to dress it up? The corral shown holds three good-sized trash cans, concealing them without making them inaccessible.

The design calls for the corral to be placed next to a building, fence, or wall, so there are slats (similar to those in a picket fence or those surrounding a deck) on three sides, and a simple series of horizontal rails in back. If your corral will be visible on all four sides, simply continue the slats across the back. You may even be able to convince your trash service to put the cans back in the corral after they are emptied. Then you could place the corral out near the end of your driveway and never have to worry about taking the trash cans out to the curb and bringing them in again. (This can be a great convenience when the trash is collected on days when there isn't anyone home.) With a little creative landscaping, the corral could easily become an attractive backdrop for a garden. You could even incorporate other curbside conveniences such as a light or a mailbox into the corral's design. 🍃

MAKING THE CORRAL

Build the base first, then put the walls on top of that. You may want to use pressure-treated wood for the base. ❀

HAVE ON HAND:

- Tape measure
- Square
- Circular saw
- Hammer
- Screw gun/drill
- 16d nails
- 1¼- and 1⅝-inch screws
- Wood glue
- 10-foot-long 2x4
- 8-foot-long 2x4
- Two 12-foot-long 1x6s
- Eight 8-foot-long 1x4s
- Thirty-two 3-foot-long 2x2s
- Two 10-foot-long 1x3s
- Paint and paintbrush

Cutting List:
- Two runners: 6-foot-long 2x4s
- Three crosspieces: 21-inch-long 2x4s
- Four decking pieces: 6-foot-long 1x6s
- Eight posts: 31-inch-long 1x4s
- Five long horizontals: 6-foot-long 1x3s
- Four short horizontals: 22½-inch-long 1x3s
- 32 slats: 31-inch-long 2x2s
- 1x3 rails: front, 75½ inches; back, 70⁵⁄₁₆ inches; sides, 27½ inches

1

Cut the 2 x 4s for the runners and crosspieces to length, then nail them together to form a 2 x 6-foot frame.

2

Measure diagonals of frame to check for square. Adjust if necessary. Cut decking to length and screw pieces down with gaps in between.

3

Cut the verticals to length. Screw them together in pairs to make L-shaped corners, then screw one L to each corner of the frame.

4

Glue and screw horizontals inside the verticals. Upper pieces should be flush with the top; lower ones should be an inch above the deck.

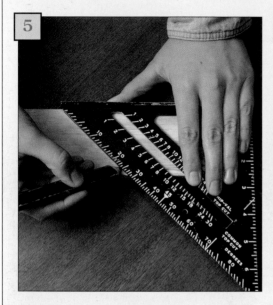

Miter the corners of the rail pieces to cut them to length. Guide your saw along a speed square to make an accurate cut.

Screw the rails to the top of the corral. The inside edges of the rails should be flush with the inside edges of the horizontal pieces.

Screw the slats to the horizontal pieces, with about 1 1/2 inches between the slats. The back gets an extra horizontal instead of slats.

Paint the corral, then set it in place. You'll find it easier to level if you place a flat cement block under each corner.

HERE'S HOW

KEEPING WEEDS AT BAY

It is all too easy for weeds to grow up around your can corral, creating a real maintenance headache. To keep the area clear, put down a layer of landscape fabric (even a layer of old newspaper will work), then cover it with a layer of mulch or gravel. This should discourage weed growth. Plant a low-maintenance ground cover such as pachysandra around the perimeter of the corral as a finishing touch.

Alternatives

A BIRDSEED CORRAL

With a style that may remind you of the feed bins in an old-time general store, this outdoor cabinet/ corral can conceal two 30-gallon trash cans full of birdseed. In addition to concealing the cans from view, the corral offers some protection against rodents (installing a latch to keep the doors shut and storing the seed in metal cans will also help discourage unwanted diners). The sloping front of the corral makes it easy to reach the contents and helps to keep the top of the corral clear. Inside the corral, the various scoops that you'll need to fill the feeders are conveniently placed above the cans.

To get the cans in and out, both the doors and part of the top are hinged and fold out of the way. The entire corral is bottomless, which makes it easy to lift the corral up and out of the way to clean up after the inevitable spill. A corral of a similar design would also be handy in a garden shed to hold bins of seed or fertilizer. Like the generator cover at the right on this page, the bin is made from T1-11 plywood with solid wood trim and reinforcing blocks. It is painted with a high-quality exterior paint to protect it from the weather. 🌺

A GENERATOR COVER

Many of our outdoor appliances are convenient to own but not very easy to move or attractive to look at. Some examples of these are generators, outdoor grills, and pumps. By building a cover for them, you can dress up your garden and protect your equipment at the same time.

The cover shown fits over a generator that is kept on a porch, where it can easily provide power in case of an emergency. While the porch roof offers some protection for the generator from the elements, the cover completely shelters the generator both from the weather and from curious young hands. With this design, the generator is completely hidden from sight, yet ready for use in a matter of seconds.

When the occasion arises, just raise the lid and slide the front panel up and off, and the generator is ready to go. There is even an extension cord waiting to be plugged in. Should the generator need servicing, the entire cover can easily be lifted off and set aside—it has no bottom. The cover is made from T1-11 plywood with solid wood used for the trim and braces. It is painted with an exterior paint in a neutral, unobtrusive color. 🌺

Building a Potting Bench

Even the simplest task can be a bear to accomplish if you don't have the right tools. This is particularly true for gardening. You wouldn't want to turn a garden over without a spade, so why should you try to pot plants and get seeds started in flats without a proper potting setup? Sure, it can be done. But once you have the proper setup, you will be amazed at how much easier potting is and how much more you will be able to get accomplished.

At the heart of a good potting setup is a potting bench—a medium-sized workbench where you can spread out your tools and materials and get to work. The bench shown here does all this and more. It features an ample, 2 x 4-foot workspace and a large shelf underneath for storing bags of potting soil and empty pots and trays. You can hang your tools from hooks driven into the bench's aprons. The painted surface resists stains and spills and cleans up easily when you are finished. Build yourself a potting bench soon—once you start using it, you'll wonder why you waited so long. ❧

BUILDING THE BENCH

The bench here is designed for gardening, but it can serve as a regular workbench as well. For added strength, make the top from tongue-and-groove 2 x 6 boards. 🌺

HAVE ON HAND:

- ► Tape measure
- ► Square
- ► Circular saw
- ► Screw gun/drill
- ► Wood glue
- ► Sandpaper
- ► ¼-inch, 3½-inch-long carriage bolts with washers and nuts
- ► 1⅝- and 3-inch screws
- ► Wrench
- ► Clamps
- ► Five 8-foot-long 2x4s
- ► ¾-inch AC plywood, 4 x 4 feet

- ► 8-foot-long 1x8

Cutting List:

- ► Four legs: 34-inch-long 2x4s
- ► Four short stretchers: 23-inch-long 2x4s
- ► Four long stretchers: 45-inch-long 2x4s
- ► Top: 24 x 48-inch plywood
- ► Shelf: 20 x 48-inch plywood
- ► Back: 48-inch-long 1x8
- ► Two sides: 16-inch-long 1x8s

Glue and screw side stretchers to legs. Locate lower stretchers 4 inches up from the ends of the legs, and upper stretchers flush with tops.

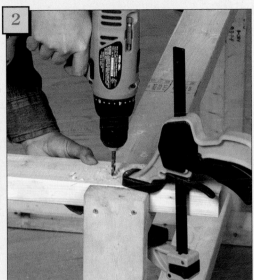

Clamp long stretchers to legs while you work. Drill two ¼-inch holes through legs into stretchers at each joint. Glue and bolt stretchers.

Cut the top to size. Set it in place—it should be flush with the legs on the sides and in the back. Screw the top down to the stretchers.

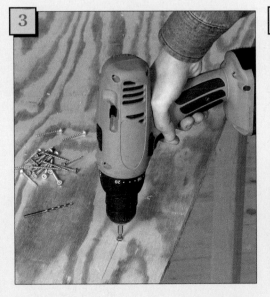

Cut the shelf to fit under the table. Slide it in place between the legs and screw it down.

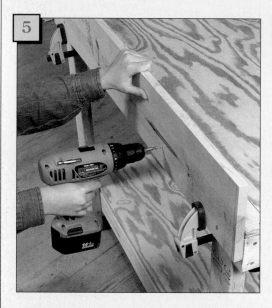

Clamp the back to the bench with spring clamps to hold it 4½ inches above the surface while you work. Glue and screw it in place.

Lay out the taper on the side pieces. The pieces should run from 4 inches wide at the narrow end to full width 2 inches from the opposite end.

Cut along layout lines with a circular saw. Clamp the pieces so that sides and back meet at the corners. Sand the sawn edge to smooth it.

Screw the sides in place. Give the entire bench a coat or two of paint or polyurethane to protect it from the soil and water you'll be using.

HERE'S HOW

AN OUTDOOR SINK

An outdoor sink is another handy addition to a potting shed, allowing you to clean up your produce right away and keep a lot of the mess out of your house. To install the sink, attach a Y-shaped nozzle to your outdoor faucet. Run a hose from one side of the faucet to another spigot over the sink. The sink itself doesn't have to be anything special—an old laundry tub or utility sink will do. When cold weather comes, simply disconnect the hose and drain the water from the line. For the drain, run a pipe from the sink's drain to a place on your property that could use a little extra water. This shouldn't be a problem with any health or building codes, as you're essentially just draining hose water, but check with your local building department to be sure.

Alternatives

A KNOCKDOWN POTTING BENCH

Even if you are pressed for space, you can still enjoy the benefits of a convenient potting bench. The design shown here provides an ample work area when it is set up but folds down practically flat against the wall when it is not needed. It could easily be installed in a garage or on one wall of a small garden shed. You might even consider hanging this bench on an outside wall or anyplace where it is convenient to get your work done. The bench can also serve as a general-duty workbench, handling all sorts of household maintenance projects.

The design is simple. You first attach the plywood bench surface to a length of 2 x 3 wood with a piano hinge. The 2 x 3 is attached to another piece of plywood, which in turn is screwed to the wall. When the surface is in working position, its weight is supported directly by the 2 x 3, not the hinges. Underneath, two folding arms swing out to hold the surface level. These are attached by lengths of piano hinge to the plywood that is fastened to the wall. All of the wood and plywood pieces should be primed and then painted with a good-quality exterior paint to enable the bench to hold up to the elements. ❧

SOIL SIFTER AND MIXING TRAY

Two accessories that you might want to build to accompany your potting bench are a soil sifter and a mixing tray. The soil sifter refines the soil, breaking up clumps and filtering out large pebbles and other debris. It is very quick and easy to make. Screw together a shallow frame, then staple a piece of ¼-inch mesh hardware cloth to the underside. The exact size is not critical. Although any type of wood will do, the sifter shown here is made from scraps of cedar, which looks nice and holds up well.

A mixing tray comes in handy when you are putting together a batch of potting mix, combining ingredients such as compost, commercial soilless seed starter, sand, and soil. The tray contains the mess, so your potting bench stays relatively clean. The size of the tray is up to you. The one shown here is approximately 24 inches long and 18 inches wide. Use whatever scraps you have available. The most important dimension is the tray's depth. You want to make it deep enough so you can mix a reasonable amount of the ingredients without having them spill all over the place. The tray shown is 4 inches deep at the front and 8 inches deep at the back. ❧

A Garden Hose Holder

Few things are more useful to a gardener than a good garden hose. But when not in use, garden hoses aren't the most attractive things in the world, nor are they particularly easy to store. A hose reel is a good solution, but the better ones are quite expensive, and the more affordable ones just don't hold up. Another solution is to build a good-looking hose hanger like the one here.

This hose holder has a wide, gentle arch you can coil the hose over without kinking it and two shelves underneath to hold accessories such as sprayers and sprinkler heads. The medallion on the front functions both as a decoration and as a stop to keep the hose from falling off the holder.

The holder is made from cedar, which will eventually weather to a silvery gray color. You could also paint it to match the colors of your home. If you often use more than one hose, you may want to build several holders. Hang them on the wall near the spigot so your hoses will be ready when needed. ❧

BUILDING THE HOLDER

The hose holder is quite straight-forward to build. You should decide which accessories you want to keep on the two shelves before you begin and adjust the sizes of the holder's parts to meet their requirements. ❧

HAVE ON HAND:

- ▶ Tape measure
- ▶ Circular saw
- ▶ Square
- ▶ Coping saw or saber saw
- ▶ Screw gun/drill and bits
- ▶ Block plane
- ▶ 1⅝-inch deck screws
- ▶ 2½-inch deck screws
- ▶ 4d galvanized finish nails
- ▶ 8-foot-long cedar 1 x 6

Cutting List:

- ▶ Two sides: 14½-inch-long 1 x 6s
- ▶ Two shelves: 5⅛-inch-long 1 x 6s
- ▶ Two supports: ¾ x 1¼ x 5⅛ inches
- ▶ Two ribs: ¾ x 4 x 15¾ inches
- ▶ Twenty-five slats: ¾ x ¾ x 6¼ inches
- ▶ Medallion: ¾ x 4¾ x 8 inches

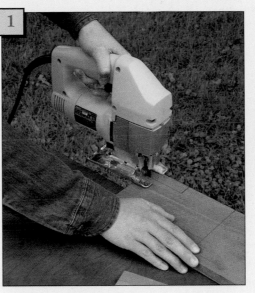

Cut all the pieces to the sizes indicated. Lay out and cut a ¾ x 3¼-inch notch in each side to receive the back rib.

Screw a support flush with the back edge of each shelf. The ends of the supports should also be flush with the ends of the shelves.

Screw shelves in place in between the sides. The lower shelf should be ¾ inch from the bottom; the upper shelf 7⅝ inches from the bottom.

Lay out the curve on one rib with a thin strip of wood (have someone else trace it), and cut curve with a saber saw. Cut similar curve in other rib.

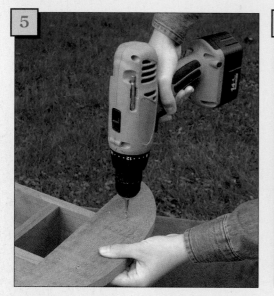

Screw the back rib in the notches you cut in the side assembly in Step 1, making sure to center the rib from side to side. Attach the front rib.

Start at the ends and nail the slats to the ribs. When you have five center slats left, test the fit. Trim each slat with a block plane if necessary.

HERE'S HOW

AVOID BURST PIPES

Even if you have a frostproof outside spigot, it can still freeze—and burst your pipes—if water is trapped inside it. Water will be trapped there and freeze if you forget to unhook your hose from the spigot. As part of your late autumn chores, make sure you disconnect the hose and drain it before you store it.

Lay out medallion so it tapers to 1¾ inches at one end. Sketch in the curve, then cut the piece to shape. Screw medallion to the front rib.

Install the hose holder by driving screws through the shelf supports into the side of your house or deck near your outside faucet.

Alternatives

A BASKET BY ANOTHER NAME

Gardeners have long known that a shallow basket can be an invaluable tool for collecting the day's harvest of vegetables, bringing them to a hose or spigot to wash, and carrying them into the kitchen. Such a basket is also handy for keeping your gloves and a few tools to take out to the garden. One style of this basket is called a trug. If you have been doing without one, you'll be pleasantly surprised at the convenience one offers. No more juggling cucumbers or kinking the stems of your daffodils. A trug provides a handy place for transporting all sorts of garden items.

You may be able to find a shallow basket that can serve as a trug in a wicker or craft store. You might even want to try weaving one yourself. Many of the larger craft stores sell both basket-making supplies and basket-making kits. The trug shown is made from thin strips of oak that are approximately 1 inch wide. If you decide to make a trug on your own, first soak thin strips of wood in warm water to make them pliable enough to bend. If this isn't enough, you can steam the strips over a pot of boiling water. Then weave the strips together—over one, under the next, and so on—to form the basket. 🌿

AN AUXILIARY SPIGOT

If your garden is some distance from your house, or if you have a large piece of property with a lot of separate garden spaces, it can be a real nuisance to run a hose out to where you need water. One convenient solution is to install an auxiliary spigot just where it's needed.

It's quite easy to install a seasonal spigot that you can drain and shut off when the ground begins to freeze. Dig a trench (trenching machines are available from most tool rental shops) about 3 to 4 inches deep—just deep enough to cover a length of hose. Purchase heavy-duty garden hose, labeled for use underground, and run it to the site of your spigot. Pitch the hose so it runs slightly downhill toward your house, and install a drain and shutoff valve in the basement where the pipe enters. This will enable you to drain the pipe and shut it off before winter's freezing temperatures arrive.

Construct a box about 3 feet tall of 1 x 4s. Before attaching the last side, fasten the hose inside the box with pipe straps. Drill a hole in the front side for a spigot.

Use a posthole digger to make a 1-foot-deep hole in the ground, and set the box in the hole with the hose attached. Cap the box with a "roof," sloped slightly to shed rain. 🌿

Constructing a Compost Bin

Making compost is a gardening fundamental. This recycling of lawn and garden by-products into a rich, crumbly substance is both an art and a science that you can pursue as actively or passively as you please. If you have the time and energy, you can turn your compost pile every two or three days and have finished compost in as little as five or six weeks. Or you can let nature take its course and have compost in several months.

While you can make compost simply and easily by building a pile in a corner of your yard, many people prefer to use a bin because it contains the mess and looks better. The advantage of the compost bin shown here is that it is portable. When it is empty, you can move it around your yard to wherever you need it. The bin is also very convenient to use, because you can unfasten one of its corners, open the entire bin, and get at the good stuff inside. Build several bins so that you can stagger your production to make sure that you always have compost when you need it. 🍃

BUILDING THE BIN

Building the compost bin is mainly a matter of drilling a lot of holes in the slats, then threading the slats onto lengths of threaded rod. The holes are oversized so that you can easily push the rods through, but you should place them as accurately as possible to make assembling the bin go smoothly. ❧

HAVE ON HAND:

- ▶ Tape measure
- ▶ Circular saw
- ▶ Electric drill with ½-inch bit
- ▶ Adjustable wrenches
- ▶ Four threaded rods: ⅜ x 26 inches
- ▶ Ten ⅜-inch flat washers and nuts

- ▶ Steel rod: ⁵⁄₁₆ x 36 inches
- ▶ Twenty-four 8-foot-long 2 x 2s, pressure treated

Cutting List:
- ▶ Forty-eight slats: 40-inch-long 2 x 2s
- ▶ Twenty-four spacers: 3-inch-long 2 x 2s

Cut the slats to length. Drill two ½-inch holes in each slat. The holes should be centered 2 inches in from each end.

Drill a third ½-inch hole in half of the slats. Center this hole 4 inches in from one end.

Cut spacers from offcuts from the slats. Drill a ½-inch hole through the center of each spacer.

Thread a nut and washer onto one end of each rod. Stack slats on rods at three corners, leaving ends with extra holes unattached at one corner.

Add spacers between slats with extra sets of holes at the corner. Fasten each stack with rods as in Step 4, using the extra holes.

Grasp the end of the 5/16-inch rod in a vise, and bend it around into a loop to make a handle.

Slide the 5/16-inch rod down through the holes at the unbolted corner. Use the loop handle to open the sides when needed.

Place bin on top of freshly dug earth. Fill it with alternating layers of high-nitrogen and high-carbon materials (see box at right).

HERE'S HOW

LOADING A COMPOST BIN

The best compost comes from mixing together a variety of different materials. As you build the stack, try to make alternate layers of high-nitrogen materials (such as grass clippings, animal manure, and kitchen scraps) and high-carbon materials (such as straw, cornstalks, and leaves). You can also add limited amounts of soil supplements such as ground limestone and rock phosphate. As a general rule of thumb, aim for a 3:1 ratio of high-carbon to high-nitrogen material.

Alternatives

A PERMANENT COMPOST BIN

If you prefer to keep your compost bin in a set location, such as an isolated spot on the edge of your property, you might want to build the bin in place. A three-sided bin like the one shown has plenty of room for garden waste, and the open side allows you easy access for loading, turning, and finally reclaiming your compost. The bin also has a slight upward flair both for appearance and to accommodate bulky trimmings before they are composted. This bin was made with pressure-treated lumber, and it will last for years outside with little or no upkeep.

Start your bin by digging holes for the corner posts. Place the centers of the holes about 4 feet apart. The holes should be at least 2 feet deep to give the posts a secure footing. Place the posts in the holes and brace them in position by gradually filling the soil back while making sure the posts stay upright. Attach the side pieces to the posts. On the open side, add a second set of uprights, sandwiching the side pieces between them and the posts to give the opening added support. Backfill the holes to hold the posts securely in place. As a final decorative touch, cut a shallow point at the top of each post. ✿

PURCHASED COMPOST BINS

Many garden centers and supply catalogs carry a variety of compost bins that will do the same job as a bin you make yourself. They are generally made of a tough, weather-resistant plastic in a dark color. The dark coloring helps absorb heat from the sun, which hastens the composting process.

There are two basic styles of these premade bins: top-loading hoppers, like the one shown, and tumbling drums. The hopper styles usually hold a little more material than the drums, but the drums tend to break down material into compost a little bit faster. The reason that the drums work faster is that they can be tumbled or rolled around. This process aerates the mix for faster decomposition. You can accomplish the same thing in a hopper-style composter by mixing the materials inside every few days with a digging fork.

If you are thinking of buying a composter, there are a few key features you should look for. The bin should have some means of ventilation, as too much heat can kill off the aerobic composting action. It should be relatively easy to load and unload. Look for a model that tips or that has a lower door for the easiest possible unloading. ✿

Building a Cold Frame

When the cold, dark days of winter seem to stretch out endlessly in front of you, building a cold frame may chase away the wintertime blues. A cold frame is essentially a small greenhouse that can give you a several-week head start on the growing season. You can even turn the cold frame into a hot bed by running an electric line out to it and burying a heating cable in the ground below. (Make sure the cable is rated for burial before you install it.)

The cold frame pictured makes use of plastic wood, a wood substitute that is made from recycled plastic and wood by-products. It is impervious to rot and never needs painting, and its dark color helps absorb some needed warmth from the sun. The lid of the cold frame is a used window sash. Though you can use the sash with the original glass in place, it is safer to replace it with either acrylic (Plexiglas) or polycarbonate plastic (Lexan). Both are easy to use and available from most hardware stores.

Toward the end of the season, plants may grow so tall that it's hard to close the lid completely without damaging them. Partially closed, however, the cold frame still offers good protection, especially if you throw a protective covering over it. ❧

ASSEMBLING THE COLD FRAME

Acquire the window sash before you begin, then build your cold frame to size. Used window sashes are frequently free for the asking from remodeling contractors. Be sure that the sashes do not contain lead-based paint or window putty. ❧

HAVE ON HAND:

- Tape measure
- Circular saw
- Screw gun/drill and bits
- Speed square
- Chalk line
- 2-inch screws
- 3-inch screws
- Hinges
- Window sash, 27 x 33 inches
- Two 8-foot-long pieces of 2 x 6 plastic wood

Cutting List:

- Six sides: 30-inch-long pieces of 2 x 6 plastic wood
- Two corner blocks: 1½ x 1½ x 9 inches
- Hinge bar: 1½ x 1½ x 33 inches

Cut all six side pieces to length. Screw four of the pieces together to form a frame. Predrill the holes to avoid breaking the screws.

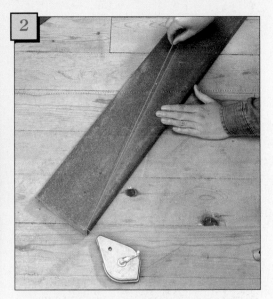

Snap a chalk line from corner to corner on one of the remaining side pieces to make the sloped side pieces. Cut along the line.

Tilt the blade on your circular saw to match the angle of the sloped sides. Trim the edge of the remaining side piece to match the sides.

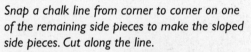

Screw the sloped sides to the side you beveled in Step 3. Attach this 3-sided frame to the 4-sided frame using blocks in the corners.

Finish attaching the upper frame to the lower by driving screws down through the sloped sides. Predrill holes to avoid splitting the material.

Set sash in place on frame assembly. It should overhang about ¼ inch along the bottom edge. Cut hinge bar to fill in the gap at top.

Attach the hinges to the hinge bar and the sash. Use hinges with removable pins so you can remove the sash when the weather turns warm.

Place the cold frame in your garden and use it to get a head start on the growing season. Cut a stick to prop the sash open on warm days.

HERE'S HOW

TENDING TO A COLD FRAME

Gardening under a cold frame isn't a hands-off operation. You'll need to monitor the temperature inside the frame and make adjustments accordingly. As the daytime temperatures rise and the sun begins to really do its job, you'll need to prop the lid open to avoid cooking your crop prematurely. Then, as the sun goes down, you'll have to remember to close the box up to retain the heat. You'll have to experiment a bit to find the right times of day for opening and closing. Also, remember to water the plants inside as needed—the window sash will keep most of the rain away from the plants.

You can also purchase and install thermal sash openers. These require no electricity. Springs that open and close the frame are triggered by a thermostatic device. The cold frame gets the proper ventilation without your doing a thing. You still have to be sure to water, however.

Alternatives

A PURCHASED COLD FRAME

If you are not inclined to build your own cold frame, you can still reap the benefits of cold-frame gardening by purchasing a commercially manufactured unit. These cold frames are made from durable, extruded aluminum rails with acrylic (Plexiglas) or polycarbonate (Lexan) plastic panels instead of glass. Plastic-paneled units are lighter than those with glass panels, but they can become scratched. If using glass, find a cold frame with insulated glass panels. Like regular glass, these panels will allow the sunlight through. In addition, they help retain some of that heat overnight.

Another approach is to use row covers to protect your plants. These fabric covers are supported by a series of wire hoops that hold the covers up off the plants. Row covers can provide protection throughout the growing season. During times when frost threatens, they can offer frost protection down to 28°F. During warmer months, the right row cover can protect your plants from insects and from the effects of too much sun and heat. They also can serve as a windbreak to protect fragile transplants until they have a chance to adjust to their new environment. 🌸

A VARIETY OF GREENHOUSES

The next step up from a cold frame is a greenhouse. These can range from a windowlike box that takes the place of one of the windows in your house to a freestanding outbuilding with its own plumbing and heating systems. Somewhere in between are sunrooms and add-on greenhouses like the one shown in the photo. While a cold frame can extend the growing season for your gardening, a greenhouse can make gardening a year-round affair.

The different styles of greenhouses have advantages and disadvantages. Obviously, the bigger the size of the greenhouse that you want, the more it will cost. But bigger greenhouses allow you to pursue more options when it comes time to plant. Greenhouses that are attached to your house are very convenient as you have immediate access to them and they can share the house's existing mechanical systems. But they can also cause trouble by losing a lot of heat in winter (or gaining it in summer), and you may have trouble with excess humidity. A freestanding structure isolates the greenhouse environment from your home, but you need to install separate mechanical systems for it. 🌸

Glossary

AGGREGATE the ingredients in concrete that make up the majority of its bulk. Concrete usually has coarse aggregate (stones) and fine aggregate (sand).

ARBOR a structure designed as a support for vines and other plants.

BACKSAW a handsaw with a thin blade reinforced by a thick metal stiffener. Used primarily for making straight, accurate crosscuts in wood.

BLOCK PLANE a relatively small hand tool with a flat sole and a sharp blade that protrudes slightly through that sole. Used for trimming wood surfaces flat and flush to one another.

BUTT JOINT a joint where one piece is simply run into the second without any type of interlock or overlap.

CARRIAGE BOLT a mechanical fastener with a domed, round head. The underside of the head has a square section that bites into the surrounding wood, preventing the bolt from turning as its adjoining nut is tightened.

CEMENT an ingredient in concrete that binds the other ingredients together.

CIRCULAR SAW a hand-held power tool with a circular blade, very useful for making straight cuts.

COMBINATION SQUARE a metal tool consisting of a straight blade/ruler attached to a movable head. One side of the head is square to the blade, the other is at a 45-degree angle. Used for marking layout lines and checking assemblies for square.

COMPOST a soil-like material made from rotted organic matter (such as grass clippings and leaves). Used as a fertilizer and soil conditioner.

CONCRETE a mixture of water, cement, and coarse and fine aggregates, which starts as a liquid then sets to a rocklike material.

COPING SAW a handsaw with a handle attached to a C-shaped metal frame. A thin blade is held under tension by the frame. Used for making intricate cuts in wood.

COUNTERSINK the process of driving a screw into a surface so its head is flush with that surface. Also, a drill bit used to create a recess for the screwhead.

CROSSCUT to cut a board across the grain.

DECK SCREWS wood screws that have a weather-resistant coating or are made of a material, such as stainless steel, that resists rust.

ELECTRIC DRILL/DRIVER a hand-held power tool capable of drilling holes or driving screws. Can be battery powered or corded. Often has a variable speed control.

EYEBOLT a mechanical fastener with a loop to which ropes and chains can be attached.

FORM a mold into which wet concrete is poured. Can be made in almost any shape.

FRAMING LUMBER lumber that is generally used for building houses. Usually 1½ inches thick (nominally 2 inches) and 4, 6, 8, 10, or 12 inches wide.

FRAMING SQUARE an L-shaped piece of steel or aluminum with the legs at 90 degrees to each other. One leg is usually 24 inches long, and the other 18 inches.

GRAVEL MIX a type of prebagged concrete that uses both sand and gravel as aggregate. It is stronger than sand mix, and can be used for all concrete applications.

LAP JOINT a type of wood joint where part of one of the adjoining pieces overlaps part of the other piece.

MITER a type joint where the ends of the pieces to be joined are cut at matching angles (usually 45 degrees).

MITER BOX a device made to guide a saw at a specific angle. It is generally used for cutting miters.

MITER GAUGE a device used on the table saw to guide boards past the blade when crosscutting. It usually runs in a slot in the saw's table.

NAIL SET a punch used to drive the head of a nail below the surface of a board.

PHILLIPS SCREWDRIVER a screwdriver with an X-shaped tip, used for driving Phillips-head screws.

PILOT HOLE a hole drilled for a screw that is smaller than the screw's diameter so the screw's threads have material to bite into.

PREBAGGED CONCRETE concrete that comes with the basic ingredients (cement, coarse aggregate, and fine aggregate) premeasured and mixed together in 60-pound bags. The user has only to add water to hydrate the mix.

PREDRILL to drill pilot holes for screws and/or nails. Generally done to avoid splitting the pieces being fastened.

PRESSURE-TREATED LUMBER lumber that has been treated with chemicals (usually chromated-copper arsenate, known as CCA) to inhibit rot.

PRIMER a paint product used to coat raw wood that promotes better adhesion of top coats. Usually white or gray.

RABBET a square step cut in the edge of a piece of wood.

RAISED BED a garden where the planting surface is elevated above the surrounding area. Usually surrounded by some sort of barrier to contain the soil.

REBAR steel rods that are embedded in concrete to give the concrete added strength.

RIP CUT to cut a board parallel to its grain.

RIP FENCE a device used on the table saw to guide a board past the blade when cutting with the grain. The distance between the blade and the fence determines the width of the board.

SABER SAW a hand-held power tool that uses a straight, reciprocating blade to make cuts. Very useful for cutting along curves. Also known as a jigsaw.

SAND MIX a type of prebagged concrete that uses only sand as aggregate. Not as strong as gravel mix, though it works better for thin applications (less than 2 inches thick).

SLATS a series of thin strips of wood similar to the pickets in a fence.

SLIDING T-BEVEL a tool with an adjustable blade used for marking and transferring angles. Also called a bevel square.

SPEED SQUARE a triangular-shaped tool used for marking 90-degree cuts across boards.

STOVE BOLT a mechanical fastener with a round head, whose threads run the full length of the shank.

STRAIGHT SCREWDRIVER a screwdriver with a flat tip used for driving straight-slotted screws. Also called a slotted screwdriver.

TABLE SAW a stationary woodworking machine consisting of a rectangular table with a circular saw blade projecting through the center. Used for ripping and crosscutting lumber.

TOP COAT the final coat (or coats) of paint.

TRELLIS a latticework structure used as a support for growing vines.

TRY SQUARE a relatively small L-shaped tool, generally with a metal blade attached to a wooden handle. Used for marking square layouts and checking assemblies for square.

Index

TIME® LIFE BOOKS

Time-Life Books is a division of Time Life Inc.
Time-Life is a trademark of Time Warner Inc. and affiliated companies.

TIME LIFE INC.
CHAIRMAN AND CHIEF EXECUTIVE OFFICER: Jim Nelson
PRESIDENT AND CHIEF OPERATING OFFICER: Steven Janas
SENIOR EXECUTIVE VICE PRESIDENT AND CHIEF OPERATIONS OFFICER:
   Mary Davis Holt
SENIOR VICE PRESIDENT AND CHIEF FINANCIAL OFFICER: Christopher Hearing

TIME-LIFE BOOKS
PRESIDENT: Larry Jellen
SENIOR VICE PRESIDENT, NEW MARKETS: Bridget Boel
VICE PRESIDENT, HOME AND HEARTH MARKETS: Nicholas M. DiMarco
VICE PRESIDENT, CONTENT DEVELOPMENT: Jennifer L. Pearce

TIME-LIFE TRADE PUBLISHING
VICE PRESIDENT AND PUBLISHER: Neil S. Levin
SENIOR SALES DIRECTOR: Richard J. Vreeland
DIRECTOR, MARKETING AND PUBLICITY: Inger Forland
DIRECTOR OF TRADE SALES: Dana Hobson
DIRECTOR OF CUSTOM PUBLISHING: John Lalor
DIRECTOR OF RIGHTS AND LICENSING: Olga Vezeris

GARDEN ACCENTS
DIRECTOR OF NEW PRODUCT DEVELOPMENT: Carolyn M. Clark
NEW PRODUCT DEVELOPMENT MANAGER: Lori A. Woehrle
SENIOR EDITOR: Linda Bellamy
DIRECTOR OF DESIGN: Kate L. McConnell
PROJECT EDITOR: Jennie Halfant
TECHNICAL SPECIALIST: Monika Lynde
DIRECTOR OF PRODUCTION: Carolyn Bounds
QUALITY ASSURANCE: Jim King and Stacy L. Eddy

Printed in U.S.A.
10 9 8 7 6 5 4 3 2 1

Produced by Storey Communications, Inc.
Pownal, Vermont

President	Pamela B. Art
Director of Custom Publishing	Megan Kuntze
Editorial Director	Margaret J. Lydic
Art Director	Cindy McFarland
Project Manager	Gwen W. Steege
Book Editors	Larry Shea and Molly Jackel
Horticultural Editor	Charles W.G. Smith
Photo Coordination	Giles Prett, Cici Mulder, Erik Callahan, Laurie Figary
Book Design	Jonathon Nix/Verso Design
Art Direction	Mark A. Tomasi
Photo Stylist	Sheri Lamers
Production and Layout	Jennifer A. Jepson Smith
Indexer	Peggy Holloway
Author	Ken Burton
Primary Photography	Kevin Kennefick

Additional photography on pages, as follows: Gay Bumgarner/Positive Images (63 left, 113 right); Karen Bussolini/Positive Images (49 right); California Redwood Association (37 right, 53 left); Walter Chandoha (53 right, 97 right, 127 left); Donna Chiarelli (89 right, 94, 119 right); Cornell Laboratory of Ornithology (71 right top, 71 right bottom, 71 right lower middle, 71 left); R. Todd Davis (97 left); Alan & Linda Detrick (131 right); Derek Fell (iv, 28, 37 left, 79 right, 113 left, 135 right); Roger Foley (6, 101 left); Harry Haralambou (33 left, 89 left); Holt Studios International (114, 131 left); Jerry Howard/Positive Images (41 left); Jerry Pavia (8, 41 right); Donna and Tom Krischan (101 right); Allan Mandell (58); Giles Prett/Storey Communications, Inc. (127, 135 left); Rob & Ann Simpson (71 right upper middle); Mark Turner (84, 93 right); The Terry Wild Studio (33 right).

Special thanks to the following for their help: Berkshire Botanic Gardens, Stockbridge, MA; California Redwood Association, Novato, CA; Collector's Warehouse, Williamstown, MA; Equinox Valley Nursery, Manchester, VT; Ward's Nursery and Garden Center, Great Barrington, MA.

School and library distribution by Time-Life Education,
P.O. Box 85026, Richmond, Virginia 23285-5026.

CIP data available upon request:
Librarian, Time-Life Books
2000 Duke Street
Alexandria, Virginia 22314

ISBN 0-7370-0626-9

Zone Map

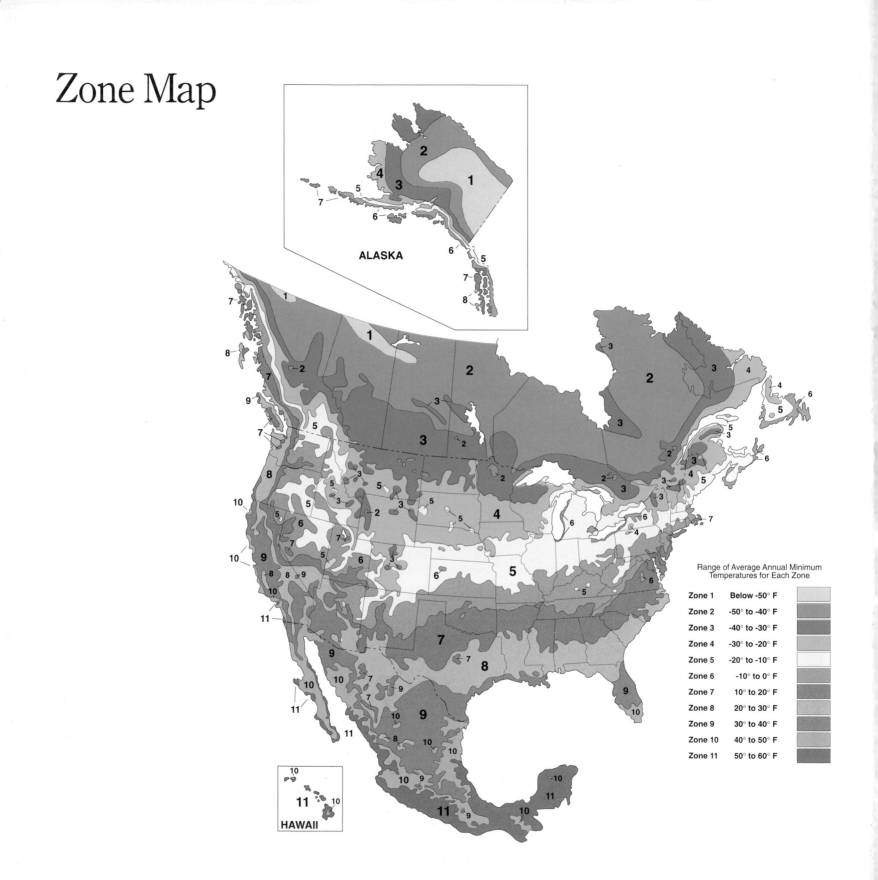

ALASKA

HAWAII

Range of Average Annual Minimum
Temperatures for Each Zone

Zone 1	Below -50° F
Zone 2	-50° to -40° F
Zone 3	-40° to -30° F
Zone 4	-30° to -20° F
Zone 5	-20° to -10° F
Zone 6	-10° to 0° F
Zone 7	10° to 20° F
Zone 8	20° to 30° F
Zone 9	30° to 40° F
Zone 10	40° to 50° F
Zone 11	50° to 60° F